Claire Denis

Contemporary Film Directors

Edited by James Naremore

The Contemporary Film Directors series provides concise, well-written introductions to directors from around the world and from every level of the film industry. Its chief aims are to broaden our awareness of important artists, to give serious critical attention to their work, and to illustrate the variety and vitality of contemporary cinema. Contributors to the series include an array of internationally respected critics and academics. Each volume contains an incisive critical commentary, an informative interview with the director, and a detailed filmography.

A list of books in the series appears at the end of this book.

Claire Denis |

Judith Mayne

**UNIVERSITY
OF
ILLINOIS
PRESS**
URBANA
AND
CHICAGO

∞ This book is printed on acid-free paper.

Library of Congress Cataloging-in-Publication Data
Mayne, Judith.
Claire Denis / Judith Mayne.
p.   cm. — (Contemporary film directors)
Filmography: p.
Includes bibliographical references and index.
ISBN 0-252-02991-7 (alk. paper)
ISBN 0-252-07238-3 (pbk. : alk. paper)
1. Denis, Claire—Criticism and interpretation.
I. Title. II. Series.
PN1998.3.D465M39   2005
791.4302'33'092—dc22   2004023669

Contents |

Near the beginning of Claire Denis's 2001 film *Trouble Every Day*, we see Coré (Béatrice Dalle), looking out the barred window of the house she shares with her husband, Léo (Alex Descas). As if following Coré's line of vision to a reverse shot, we see a woman, jauntily dressed in a beret and a scarf, jump out of a taxicab (figs. 1 and 2). It takes just a split second to realize that Coré is not watching this woman, but rather that the film is moving from the house to the city street, from Coré and Léo to another couple, Shane (Vincent Gallo) and June (Tricia Vessey). Thus we are not seeing what Coré sees, but rather the arrival in Paris of Shane and June Brown in a cab driven by the woman. Throughout the film, the parallel yet separate tracks of these two couples are explored, and this kind of cut—in which continuity is established momentarily, only to be revealed as a part of the overall pattern of contrast—is very common, not only in this film but in the cinema in general. But in that brief moment when Coré seems to be watching the cab, and watching not primarily the arrival of Shane and June but the woman taxi driver, something of the particular beauty of the films of Claire Denis can be grasped.

Coré is a prisoner in her house, and the woman who briefly appears to be the object of her gaze stands in visual contrast to her. This woman moves; she has a "nontraditional" job, and there is something appealing about her equally nontraditional choice of the appropriate clothing for the job. Coré's hunger lets loose a wildness, a savage destructive force; this woman's autonomy, however briefly it is perceived, is tame by comparison. Across the body of this woman we make a connection between Coré and the newlywed American couple. For a moment, the contrast between these two women—Coré the prisoner, and the cab driver doing her job—is also suggestive of a bond, a connection. This is a very small

Figure 1: Coré in *Trouble Every Day* |

Figure 2: The cab driver in *Trouble Every Day* |

moment, but it is one of many such moments that I remember vividly from Claire Denis's films. To be sure, the premise of *Trouble Every Day* is complex, suggesting the continuum between sexual desire and violence, and situated in a context where fear and anxiety are constant. Perhaps I remember this brief "encounter" because it is one of the few lighter moments in the film; here is a woman, seemingly caught within Coré's gaze, who is neither attacker nor prey (Shane's eye will quickly be drawn to the maid in the hotel). But I think, rather, that this is one of many examples in Claire Denis's work of how the small detail, the brief moment of connection, is never taken for granted. Upon such moments are built a fascination with human interaction and cinematic vision. Claire Denis's films teach you how to be attentive to these moments. Shortly after the arrival of Shane and June, the appearance of the nape of a woman's neck will set into motion a series of deadly desires. In other films by Denis, individuals circle each other, move through landscapes and cityscapes, to pause for a moment of connection that is all the more breathtaking for how brief it is. Daïga, the Lithuanian immigrant in *I Can't Sleep* who observes with fascination Camille, the man whom she discovers is the much sought-after killer of old women, makes physical contact with him only once. She follows him to a café, stands next to him, and asks for the sugar. When he passes it, their hands touch ever so lightly; it is almost a flutter. But the film has so patiently watched these two, and in particular has watched Daïga watch Camille, that when this moment arrives it is both poignant and momentous.

Claire Denis's films are about watching, bearing witness, and making contact. As a woman director, Denis challenges virtually every preconception about what is appropriate material. She is known as a director drawn to men, and certainly her films are often focused on a fascination with male bodies and the interactions between men, like Dah and Jocelyn, the two friends in *No Fear, No Die,* or the French Foreign Legionnaires in *Beau travail.* But Denis's films certainly demonstrate an interest in women, and often—as in the case of Béatrice Dalle's Coré in *Trouble Every Day* or Valérie Lemercier's Laure in *Friday Night*—representations of women are as challenging and engaging as the representations of men.

Denis's films are fully immersed in a world shaped and defined by the aftermath of colonization and decolonization. Denis herself grew up in several different countries in Africa, and an acute awareness of the ways in which how one looks (in both senses of the term) through the prism of race is present in all of her films. In her first feature film, *Chocolat,* a French woman returns to Cameroon and remembers her childhood there; while not all of Denis's films are so directly centered on the colonial encounter, her cinema reflects a world where people live through the complex legacies of colonialism.

My goals in the present study are, first, to explore the range of Claire Denis's career, one that is shaped by particular collaborations with actors and writers and other artists, by a love of the cinema, and by a curiosity about the ways in which people move, about how bodies perform, and how the relationship between center and margin is constantly shifting. Second, I examine her major films in detail in order to understand and appreciate Denis's remarkable cinematic vision, one in which viewers are invited to witness and to observe. As my example from *Trouble Every Day* suggests, Denis's cinema is filled with moments that may well function in relationship to the larger themes and preoccupations of a given film, but which also retain their own unique rhythm and presence.

In the first section, I examine the broad outlines of Denis's film career and suggest some of the key preoccupations of her work. I then move on to analyses of Denis's feature films. In the second section, I examine how specific forms of storytelling and visual observation occur in Denis's first two feature films, *Chocolat* (1988) and *No Fear, No Die* (1990). The third section focuses on the brother/sister relationship as it is explored in two films, *U.S. Go Home* (1994) and *Nénette and Boni* (1996). In the fourth section, I look at two intertwining themes in *I Can't Sleep* (1994) and *Beau travail* (1999–2000): the representation of the male body, and the use of the tracking shot. The last section examines the male-female couple and the city of Paris in *Trouble Every Day* (2001) and *Friday Night* (2002).

While each section is devoted to the study of particular films, all of the themes that I explore are relevant to all of Denis's work. The form of storytelling that is developed in Denis's first two feature films will be revised and extended throughout her career, but the preoccupation with witnessing and with bearing witness has been a constant in her films. The brother/sister relationship may appear to be a particular feature of *U.S. Go Home* and *Nénette and Boni,* but virtually all of Denis's films demonstrate a preoccupation with kinship, with family ties and, more often, with what takes the place of family ties. The child France's closest companion, in *Chocolat,* is the Cameroonian family servant, and while the two male leads of *No Fear, No Die* have few visible family ties, the brotherly bond between them is far stronger than the other family connections we see in the film.

Claire Denis is well known as a director who presents beautiful portraits of male bodies, and the two films that are most preoccupied with the representation of the male body, *I Can't Sleep* and *Beau travail,* are also the films most explicitly taken up with gay sexuality. In both of these films, the representation of masculinity intersects with the representation of women, for women have particularly important roles in both films in situating how we look at the male body. In more general terms, the connections between the body, gender, and sexuality inform all of Denis's films. Very much connected to the question of the body is the question of desire, and *Trouble Every Day* and *Friday Night* represent sexuality as both terrifying and liberating.

The films that I discuss are available on DVD or video (*I Can't Sleep* is officially out of print, but copies often surface on Ebay), with the exception of *U.S. Go Home.* The film was made for a French television series, and while it has been shown at film festivals and retrospectives of Denis's work, it has never been distributed in the United States. I hesitated about including discussion of a film that is so hard to see, but *U.S. Go Home* is such an important part of Denis's work that I decided to include it. I have had the opportunity to see all of Denis's films, but because most of Denis's short films are very difficult to see, and even though some of these films are remarkable achievements, I have kept discussion of them to a minimum.

My interview with Claire Denis took place in Paris in July 2003. Denis had just returned to the city and was about to leave the next day to shoot her next feature, a film inspired by Jean-Luc Nancy's book *L'Intrus* (2000), and featuring some familiar actors from Denis's films—Michel Subor, Grégoire Colin, and Béatrice Dalle. Denis discussed many of her lesser-known films, as well as the use of voice-over, cinematic influences on her work, and the importance of *I Can't Sleep* in her career. Denis is an extremely articulate commentator on her own work and on the cinema in general, and it was a privilege to meet her and to include our discussion in this volume. All of my discussions of Denis's career are drawn from published sources, interviews in particular (I have not sought verification from Denis for any of the statements or interpretations that appear in my book). All translations from the French (including the interview with Denis) are my own.

I began this project out of great love and admiration for Denis's films. While there is always some relief in the completion of a project, I have to say that I am sorry to see this one end. Mostly I am grateful to have had the opportunity to examine the beautiful, moving films of such an amazing filmmaker.

| | |

I am grateful to the College of Humanities and the Departments of French and Italian and Women's Studies at the Ohio State University for research support, and to my research assistant, Clarissa Moore. For help in finding films and for access to films, thanks to the following individuals: Florence Arrigoni Neri of Les Poissons Volants; Keith Griffiths; David Heinemann of FACSEA; Laura Marchandise of Arena Films; Dean Otto of the Walker Art Center; Grazia Quaroni of the Cartier Foundation; Paul Richer of Flach-Pyramide International; and David Schwartz of the American Museum of the Moving Image. A special thanks to Bill Horrigan and David Filipi of the Wexner Center for the Arts at OSU.

I am grateful to the staff members at the Bibliothèque du Film and the Inathèque of the Institut National de l'Audiovisuel in Paris for their help and assistance.

I thank the following friends and colleagues for their support and encouragement: Diane Birckbichler, Mitchell Greenberg, Susan Hayward, Stephen Heath, Linda Mizejewski, Dana Polan, Thibaut Schilt, Kevin Snorteland, Maurice Stevens, Ruby Tapia, Marie-Claire Vallois, and Emma Wilson. I owe special debts to B. Ruby Rich and to Marie-Pierre Macia, who proved that female networking is alive and well.

As always, my greatest debt is to Terry Moore.

Claire Denis

Seeing Others |

One of the distinctive features of Claire Denis's cinema is the attention paid to the periphery, to the seemingly insignificant detail. All of Denis's films have plots, and they certainly have characters. But the plots of her films never lead in a single direction, and they are often fragmented. The characters in Denis's films are fully present on screen, yet even when they are driven by what appears to be the weight of the past (or the present), we are never given anything resembling psychological portraits. In the opening moments of most of Denis's films, there is a wealth of visual information, and while every detail matters, it isn't always clear how. A great pleasure, as well as challenge, of Denis's cinema, is paying attention, engaging fully with the range of images and sounds presented on screen (as Elana del Rio [2003] puts it, Denis's films take "on the project of seducing us away from our 'proper' customary conduct as viewers"). It is common to describe Denis as a filmmaker "of the image," that is, a filmmaker devoted to formal innovation and aesthetic beauty rather than a story. This is a misleading description, since it suggests that filmmakers (and audiences) have to choose between the two. There is unquestionable cinematic beauty in Denis's films, but never does beauty function in some isolated realm of cinematic purity. Claire Denis's cinema is a cinema fully engaged with a complex world.

Since *Chocolat,* the 1988 film that was her feature film debut, Denis has directed seven additional narrative feature films, two feature-length documentaries, and numerous short films. Her narrative features are her best-known films, and these films will be examined later in some detail. In order to introduce and situate Claire Denis's cinema, I turn to what might be considered the "periphery" of her own career, the two feature-length documentaries that are far less well known than her fiction films. These are the only documentary films that Denis has completed, and together they give an intriguing sense of Claire Denis's approach to the art of filmmaking. Additionally, the films, while quite different in subject matter—one follows a Cameroonian musical group on its first concert tour in France; the other is a portrait of veteran filmmaker Jacques Rivette—stand together as indications of the primary themes that Claire Denis has explored in her work. And as coincidence would have it, these are the only two films in which the director makes a visible appearance.

Man No Run (1989) appeared immediately after *Chocolat,* and the film had a fairly limited release. It follows the first concert trip to France of the Cameroonian musical group Les Têtes Brûlées (the group's name means "heads on fire," which, one of the musicians explains in the film, was a risky name for an African group but one that seemed totally appropriate). The group became enormously popular in Cameroon in 1987, and Denis met the group while she was shooting *Chocolat.* The group's music is bikutsi, a traditional form of music of the Beti, an ethnic and linguistic group who are associated with the forests and villages of Cameroon, but who have also migrated to the urban center of Yaoundé (see Fuller, Fuller, and Ahanda [1997]). The Têtes Brûlées's form of bikutsi could be described as hybrid, to the extent that they use electric guitars instead of traditional African instruments. But the notion of hybridity can be misleading, implying as it does a fusion of Western and African influences. The Têtes Brûlées adapt their instruments—by, say, placing a piece of foam underneath the guitar strings—to better create the sounds of traditional African instruments, that is, to preserve bikutsi music, not to "Westernize" it.

Denis was so taken with the music of the Têtes Brûlées (she even referred to herself as a groupie [Colmant 1989: 18]) that she originally thought of having France, the female protagonist of *Chocolat*, visit a club to hear their music near the end of the film. "I kept in touch with them as I was editing *Chocolat*, and they wrote me a letter and told me they were coming to France for a tour, their first tour outside of Cameroon. So I managed to find a camera and some film stock and there we were. I didn't foresee my career. Things happen" (Romney 2000).

The title of *Man No Run* refers both to a song by the Têtes Brûlées and a slang expression, as one of the musicians explains in the film, for someone who sticks around, who stays with his comrades. Denis's film is a "concert film" only in the sense that she follows the group on their first tour to France. Equally if not more interesting is the fact that except for Jean-Marie Ahanda, the founder of the group, it was the musicians' first trip to France. Thus the film becomes a record of their impressions of France, some of which are funny, some poignant, some both. At the beginning of the film, we see the Têtes Brûlées in concert, but most of the film moves back and forth from their different concert venues—in clubs, at what appears to be a music festival, at a large amphitheater—to observations of the group when they are socializing, or resting, or seeing France for the first time. Increasingly, in the course of the film, an obvious intimacy develops, not just between the spectator and the group, but also between the musicians and Claire Denis herself.

Early in the film, the musicians arrive at Orly airport near Paris, greeted by Ahanda and Philippe Laburthe-Tolra, a French university professor who has written extensively on the Beti of southern Cameroon, and who has taught at the University of Cameroon. The voice-over (by an unidentified member of the group) refers to Laburthe-Tolra as a "white Beti," a "toasted" white person who has become one of them. When the musicians get off the plane, introductions are made all around, in a spirit of excitement and laughter. One of the musicians looks at the camera and says "Hi Claire!" We then see the group in a café, and the musicians tell of their difficulties in securing passports. The Têtes Brûlées have a very distinctive style in their appearance as well as their music.

On stage they wear bright costumes, featuring knee pads and colorful backpacks. Their bodies are painted with white stripes and dots (the film shows us the lengthy preparations required for the body-painting), and they wear sunglasses with radio antennae attached. Their heads are shaved with strategically placed tufts of hair remaining. The hair—or lack of it—is what caused the Cameroonian officials to hesitate in issuing their passports. The reason?—the officials thought the group would be an embarrassment to Africa. Eventually the group wore wigs for their passport photographs, and they were able to travel to France.

When the musicians tell the story, Laburthe-Tolra laughs and comments that the tale is *"très drôle"* (very amusing). Laburthe-Tolra doesn't appear in the film after this scene. While the professor is obviously considered a friend by the Têtes Brûlées, he also seems a bit out of place, perhaps less because he is white than because he doesn't really seem to belong to the world of music. Laburthe-Tolra looks like a conventional, average French middle-aged professional, and even though the Têtes Brûlées are not in costume, their distinct hair styles are visible (and are called attention to by the story of the passports). The professor might well appear as the first instance, in the film, of the group's encounter with French people, but he is just as interesting for what his presence suggests about a white observer, one both connected to yet obviously different from the members of the group. In this sense, the professor is a stand-in for Denis herself, and his brief presence suggests that while the film traces a narrative of Africans observing France, it also traces how a white observer watches, negotiates, and engages with that very narrative.

Approximately halfway through the film, we get a sense of how the concert tour is as exhausting as it is exhilarating when we move from a concert to the dressing room, where the musicians, still in their stage costumes, are unwinding immediately afterward. But whereas previous conversations among, and individual interviews with, the musicians have a friendly and intimate tone, here there are signs of conflict. One musician is criticized for responding in French when he has been spoken to in Beti, and for being rude to elders, and there is discussion about the possibilities the musicians have, or have not had, for meeting women. Now we have been aware of Denis as an observer in the film, particularly during the interviews, but this is the only occasion where she actually makes an appearance. We see Denis's head reflected in a mirror in the room, and the composition of the shot puts the mirror in the center, between two musicians who are seated. She is standing next to the door, through which someone leaves. We do not see her filming or speaking; she is simply present. Then she moves forward, as if moving toward the discussion taking place, but as she moves, we cut to a shot of the musicians seated against the wall. She has disappeared from the frame.

If Professor Laburthe-Tolra is a visible sign of the bridge between France and Cameroon, the role that Denis acquires is different, for she observes, patiently and quietly, out of frame. This doesn't mean that she is invisible, but rather that the mode of observation that she brings to the musicians and their music and their perceptions of France is quietly discrete, out of frame but never out of sight.

A year after the appearance of *Man No Run*, Claire Denis directed a documentary about Jacques Rivette, *Jacques Rivette, le veilleur* (*Jacques Rivette, Watchman*) for the television series *Cinéma de notre temps* (*Cinema of Our Time*). The film consists of extended interviews with Rivette by film critic Serge Daney, along with clips from Rivette's films and interview segments with Bulle Ogier, one of Rivette's preferred actors. Again, approximately halfway through the film, Claire Denis makes a brief appearance. She is seated at a table outdoors with Daney and Rivette, and the conversation has turned to Pierre Corneille's last play, *Suréna*. Rivette speaks of a famous passage in the play when Suréna contemplates the fleeting nature of life, as well as the importance of single (even if isolated) moments of happiness. After we see Denis with the two men, the camera moves to capture Rivette, but we are aware of Denis's presence, to Rivette's left, as well as Daney's, to Rivette's right, since Rivette continues to speak to both of them.

When Daney tells Rivette that he sees a connection between Corneille's play and Rivette's approach to cinema, the conversation turns to the role of curiosity. The conversation is reframed as it occurs exclusively between Daney and Rivette; Denis seems to have slipped out of the frame. But during a pause in the conversation, we hear Claire Denis's distinctive voice (somewhat hoarse, somewhat raspy) suggest that Scheherazade might well be an appropriate figure to insert into this discussion of curiosity. The camera then moves to the right to frame Denis, her hand partially covering her face, as she laughs; Daney tells Rivette that they (Daney and Denis) have a theory about the "Scheherazade syndrome." Daney explains, as the camera moves away from Denis: "Scheherazade tells stories to delay two things: her death as well as an overly intimate relationship with her commander." As curiosity again becomes the subject of conversation, the camera moves from Daney to Rivette; Denis has once again disappeared from the frame. Rivette acknowledges her with a look and a knowing shrug one more time, when he says that Scheherazade is their "patron saint." The conversation between Daney and Rivette continues, and we do not see Claire Denis again in the film.

There is something almost self-effacing about Denis's appearance in the film—she covers her face, she speaks very little, and the camera shows her only very briefly. But the fact that Denis appears at all is striking. Unlike the very brief appearances we have of the director in *Man No Run*, where her presence is more identified with the felt presence of the camera as it observes from a variety of perspectives, here Denis seems to step out from her role as filmmaker for a moment, to participate in a conversation that obviously is of vital interest to her own work as a filmmaker, but to do so in front of the camera. Janet Bergstrom describes how this brief scene "makes explicit how she had been there since the beginning, a narrator hidden from view, but with her own, independent look and intellectual position, absent from the frame but director of the discussion." Specifically, Bergstrom sees this scene as indicative of numerous aspects of Denis's cinema, including the "doubling or triangulation of vision" (2003: 72). Perhaps most strikingly, this brief interlude about Corneille and Scheherazade is also a moment of decentering, of revealing, as Bergstrom suggests, the scaffolding, the infrastructure, that makes the dialogue between two men possible. Yet in the decentering, there is also a strong identification between Denis and Rivette. The discussion of time and waiting, of curiosity, of the "contract" between the actor and the director (Rivette describes the "fiction" that takes place during the actual making of the film, a fiction that involves the bond between actor and director)—all of these elements had already been central to Denis's own work as a filmmaker, and they would become increasingly important in her career.

Claire Denis thus makes literal appearances in two documentary films that, together, suggest the broad outlines of her work as a filmmaker. On the one hand, Denis is a filmmaker whose life and art have been shaped by the ways in which Africa and France have lived complicated histories of domination and resistance, of hate and love, of dependence and autonomy. Denis's love of Africa, and of various aspects of African culture, is evident in her films, but she is also attuned to the problematic ways in which white people have shown their love for Africa. *Man No Run* could easily have become a romanticized portrait of the "exotic." But because the film is so focused on how France is a strange country, and on how the musicians narrate their own way through the country, it is, rather, a thoughtful and beautiful portrait of the music as well as of the very nature of observation itself. *Jacques Rivette, le veilleur* is obviously an homage to the director, and it is shot in such a way as to draw attention to the very process of cinematic imagination. Rivette and Daney's discussions are sometimes rambling, and often they follow several ideas at once, but they are always provocative. When Claire Denis steps in frame, one senses not only her own love for the cinema but also and especially her awareness of what lies just beyond the field of vision.

Documentary cinema is the exception, not the rule, in Claire Denis's work, and these films were made in the early years of her career. The subjects of the films seem very different, but they represent two interwoven dimensions of Denis's work. On the one hand, Denis's representations of Africa engage with basic questions of how the cinema functions in relationship to what is familiar and what is strange, and in relationship to the pleasures and dangers of looking. On the other hand, Denis's awareness of film culture and film history makes her work self-reflexive not only in terms of the cultural dimensions of looking but also in terms of what the cinema has been and what it might become. No matter what the subject of Denis's films, attention is focused on how bodies move through space and how individuals look at each other.

Man No Run and *Jacques Rivette, le veilleur* were made during the same period that Claire Denis completed her first two narrative features as well as a short film shot in the United States (*Keep It for Yourself*). *Chocolat* and *S'en Fout la mort/No Fear, No Die* (1990) are the first two installments in what Denis has called the triptych of her first three feature films, for they move away from Africa on the verge of independence portrayed in *Chocolat,* to the experience of two immigrant men (one from Benin and one from Martinique) in the outskirts of Paris in *No Fear, No Die,* to the relationship between a serial killer of West Indian origins and those who know him and/or observe him, in *J'ai pas sommeil/I Can't Sleep* (1994). Denis was completing the latter film when she began shooting *U.S. Go Home* for the series *Tous les garçons et les filles de leur âge (All the Boys and Girls of Their Age)*, and this one-hour film about a brother and a sister growing up in the 1960s has close affinities with Denis's next feature, *Nénette and Boni* (1996), with the same actors (Grégoire Colin and Alice Houri) playing the brother and sister of the film's title.

Aside from *Chocolat,* Denis's best-known film to date is *Beau travail,* released in 1999–2000. The film has received numerous awards and has appeared in countless festivals. A beautifully poetic evocation of what is unspoken in the lives of contemporary members of the French Foreign Legion stationed in the tiny African country of Djibouti, *Beau travail* shares much with Denis's previous work, for the observation of masculinity and the complex relationship between France and Africa are apparent in virtually all of her films. Yet this particular film, however many affinities it shares with Denis's previous films, brought many more viewers to her work.

Denis moved in a somewhat different direction with her next feature film, *Trouble Every Day* (2001). More elliptical than Denis's previous films (but sharing with them, nonetheless, many preoccupations), *Trouble Every Day* divided critics and provoked numerous debates about the representation of sexual violence (there are two particularly gruesome scenes in the film). Perhaps predictably, after the enormous critical success of *Beau travail,* Denis was now criticized for what was seen by many critics as a misstep. (The film also had very passionate defenders.) Her next film, and most recent feature at the time of this writing, was *Friday Night/Vendredi soir* (2002), adapted from a novel by Emmanuèle Bernheim (who coauthored the screenplay with Denis). Once again this film proved to be controversial, largely because of its slow pace; the film takes place during a huge traffic jam, and the film's heroine, played (very much against type) by Valérie Lemercier, has a one-night stand with a man (Vincent Lindon) to whom she offers a ride.

One of the most interesting aspects of Denis's career is that even though there are many preoccupations running consistently through all of her films, there are also some surprising twists and turns. In particular, making *Man No Run* and *No Fear, No Die* (1990) after the success of *Chocolat* took some viewers aback. Whether or not *Chocolat* can be considered an autobiographical or semiautobiographical film (an assertion that Denis has always questioned), it does focus on the memories of a young woman who grew up in Cameroon, and it thus certainly qualifies as a film that reflects Denis's own personal history. As a documentary and (partially) a "concert film," *Man No Run* seemed to signal a detour in Denis's career. *No Fear, No Die* appeared to be a drastic departure from the personal history evident in *Chocolat,* for it focuses on the friendship between two black male immigrants who enter into a business deal involving the training and staging of cocks for fighting. The film seemed a change not only in its subject matter but also in its style, portraying the training and fighting of the cocks at such close range as to suggest a kind of poetic documentary. But this is one of the distinctive features of Denis's work: she has enormous range, and she is not at all wedded to a particular genre—far from it. And she consistently challenges what one imagines "appropriate" or typical subject matter for a white, female director.

Claire Denis's films may share affinities with the works of other contemporary French filmmakers, and there are aspects of her work that can be considered productively in the context of contemporary women's cinema. But her work remains distinctively and stubbornly original. Claire Denis always surprises her audience, whether in moving from fiction to documentary (particularly during the first several years of her career as a director), or from one type of film to another, whether it be the "colonialism from a female point-of-view" in *Chocolat* (Strauss 1990; Portuges 1996), the road movie/concert film (*Man No Run*), or the "docudramatic" tone of *No Fear, No Die.*

Denis's documentary on Jacques Rivette was made, at Rivette's request, in the same year as *No Fear, No Die.* Denis had worked as Rivette's assistant, and given how she has often referred to Rivette as someone who was crucial in encouraging her to pursue her own career as a director, one senses that this film was a labor of love, although Denis has described how she felt "terrified" at the prospect of doing the film (Romney 2000). She has also said—as she did in relationship to *Man No Run*—that the film happened "by chance" (Romney 2000). Chance may well be a factor, but Claire Denis is a director who pursues opportunities as they arise and grab her interest, not out of some preconceived notion of what the "right" way is to proceed. "Things happen" (as Denis said about how she came to make *Man No Run* [Romney 2000]), indeed.

In other words, Denis's early career was characterized by choices that some might find curious. If it is entirely appropriate to refer to Claire Denis as a "vagabond" (as the title of Sébastien Lifshitz's documentary film [1995] about Denis does), then it is important to see the kind of cinematic choices implicit in that description. For when Claire Denis had the opportunity to make a film about a Cameroonian musical group's first tour in France, she did so, largely, one guesses, out of pure love for their music and a desire to be able to document their work, even if this meant that her work on her eagerly awaited second feature film would have to wait. And many filmmakers might shrug at the opportunity to make a film about another director, no matter how beloved, particularly given that the film was made for television.

How, then, did Claire Denis come to her particular style of cinematic observation? Claire Denis was born on April 21, 1948, in Paris, the oldest child (she has a younger sister and brother) of a French couple. Denis's father was a colonial official, yet Denis describes him as someone who believed in independence, and who "asked questions about why we were there" (Denorme and Douin 21). Denis's parents were acutely aware of their situation as white colonizers in Africa, an awareness that they obviously passed on to their children. Denis has described her parents as travelers rather than typical colonizers, as people who were open to new experiences and who did not stake their happiness on living as most French people in Africa did (Denorme and Douin 22). Denis's mother returned to Paris to give birth to her, and when Claire Denis was two months old, they returned to Africa. French families who lived in Africa as part of the colonial administration returned to France for a few months every two years. In Africa, the family moved from one colonial outpost to another, so in addition to Cameroon (the setting for *Chocolat*), Denis lived in other African countries, including Djibouti (the setting for *Beau travail*) and Burkina Faso.

Denis has spoken eloquently about her childhood in Africa, of how she loved the continent yet also realized that it was not *her* homeland: "My father was a colonial functionary, so I knew I was passing through.

I didn't lose my country, because I knew it never belonged to me. Nothing belonged to us. . . . I belonged to a country—France—that I knew nothing about" (Jousse 2002: part 1). Denis grew up in Africa when independence movements were afoot in numerous countries, and she knew, even as a child, that no matter how much she loved the countries where she lived, there was something "perverse" about the relationship between whites and blacks. She knew, for instance, that she could behave very badly around the black servants in the household, without being punished (an echo of which one sees in *Chocolat* when the child, France, clearly imitating what she sees around her and seeking to establish her own authority, orders Protée to finish a conversation and take her home) (Jousse 2002: part 1).

Denis's childhood in Africa was not just the experience of a white girl in a French colony but of a white child acutely aware of the "perversity" of those relations, at a time when the very legitimacy of colonial rule was put actively and radically into question. The war for independence in Algeria was, obviously, enormously important; later, Denis said, it was difficult for her to respond to the U.S. war in Vietnam the same way that many of her French compatriots did. For her, the war wasn't something new in world history but rather a chapter in a history with which she was already familiar (Jousse 2002: part 1).

One of the most interesting stories Denis has told about her childhood in Africa is the impact that French photographer Dominique Darbois had on her. Darbois wrote a series of illustrated books (with her own photographs) for French children (the books were translated into English as well as other languages) about the lives of children in other countries—African as well as Scandinavian, Central American, and Asian (Darbois 1955; 1957; 1960). When Darbois came to Yaoundé, where Claire Denis's family was stationed, Denis's father served as Darbois's guide. Darbois was a concentration camp survivor, and the tattooed numbers on her arm were always visible. Via Darbois, this aspect of World War II history came to Cameroon and touched Claire Denis's life. A connection was made with Europe—this "cold and ugly Europe that I didn't like." Later, Denis learned that Darbois was active in the war for Algerian independence. Darbois became what we would today call a role model for Claire Denis: "I wanted to be like her—a photographer, a solitary and independent woman" (Jousse 2002: part 1).

Denis's definitive return to France occurred when she and her sister both contracted polio and had to spend more than a year in France under medical care. Her family moved to the Parisian suburbs. At the age of thirteen, Claire Denis settled in her "homeland" and, not surprisingly, felt isolated from what was presumably her own culture. When Claire Denis describes her adolescence, three themes dominate: her sense of estrangement vis-à-vis France, particularly insofar as her relationship to Africa was concerned; her love of music; and her discovery of the cinema. If all adolescents feel estranged, it is obvious that Denis's situation, as a teenager who had known France only during brief visits and suddenly found herself living in a country that was "hers" and "not hers" at the same time, was unique. For Denis, the decolonization of Africa was not a removed historical process; it was personal. In high school, Denis felt "archaic, provincial, ashamed . . . I felt like I belonged to a different century" (Jousse 2002: part 1).

Denis found in music a grand passion, and she was particularly drawn to English and American music, especially the Yardbirds and Eric Burdon and the Animals (she has said on numerous occasions that she wanted to *be* Eric Burdon [Ancian 2002: 3]). Music was a release, an outlet for inchoate feelings of rebellion and anger. It was also a comfort. Denis said in 2002 that when she hears the Beach Boys' song "In My Room" (sung by Brian Wilson), she thinks immediately of people of her generation for whom music was a way of creating a personal space. When you need to invent your own world, she said, the first place you start is in your own room (Jousse 2002: part 2). The love of music, and the ability to identify passionately with music, is a central aspect of Denis's film work. Denis uses particular musical selections to great effect. Neil Young's mournful song "Safeway Cart," which is heard over images of the legionnaires walking in the desert in *Beau travail,* comments on what we see but, more importantly, opens up a perspective to enhance the various points of view that are central to the film. Bob Marley's "Buffalo Soldier" becomes an anthem of sorts for the character of Dah (Isaach de Bankolé) in *No Fear, No Die.* After hearing songs in a Claire Denis film, it is difficult to hear them in quite the same way again, because of the indelible connections in her films between music and the images, whether they portray certain actions (walking in the desert) or certain characters (Dah).

Denis grew to love the cinema, at first because of her mother's love of the cinema: "I discovered the cinema thanks to my mother. . . . She spoke of the cinema, of how she missed it [in Africa], so I had to see what the cinema was all about, in order to be like her" (Denorme and Douin 22). She occasionally saw films in Africa, but it was when she moved to France that Denis became an avid filmgoer. Interestingly, Denis has described the experience of spectatorship as central to what the cinema initially meant to her, rather than any particular film or filmmaker. "All of a sudden, I was no longer a prisoner, I could experience other worlds. . . . I could be a spectator in a world of adventures. When I was little, the life I led made me somewhat contemplative, and thus a spectator. . . . Being a spectator was enough for me" (Denorme and Douin 22).

Denis was interested in a variety of academic subjects—she studied Japanese, history, geography—but eventually she ended up at IDHEC (Institut des Hautes Etudes Cinématographiques), the renowned national French film school (it was replaced in 1984 by FEMIS—the Fondation Européenne des Métiers de l'Image et du Son). By this time, Denis was married to a photographer (she was married at the age of eighteen), who encouraged her to think seriously about IDHEC. Denis worked as an intern for Télé Niger, "an educational channel teaching literacy via the cinema" (Ancian 2). She applied to IDHEC and, much to her surprise, she was accepted. She considered IDHEC a completely utopian idea. "I was happy to be a spectator, I had so little self-confidence, I felt like such a pariah" (Denorme and Douin 23).

Like virtually every educational institution in France, particularly in Paris, IDHEC was affected by the student/worker demonstrations of May '68. "You had the impression that everything had to be reinvented every day. Even silly things," says Denis of the atmosphere at the film school (Denorme and Douin 23). But one senses that despite her description of her own insecurities, Denis's preferred position of spectator served her well and that with the perspective of an engaged bystander, she was able to move through the various conflicts and constituencies at IDHEC with grace. The head of IDHEC at the time was Louis Daquin, a filmmaker associated with the dreaded "Tradition of Quality" against which the New Wave filmmakers rebelled. Claire Denis has the utmost respect for him; only he, she says, could have accepted the Situationist group that was visible at IDHEC at the time (the left-wing Situationists were very much associated with the reinvention and rethinking of political protest that took place during and after May '68) (Denorme and Douin 23).

Filmmakers Philippe Garrel (*Lit de la vierge* [1969]) and Jean Eustache (best known for *La Maman et la putain* [1973]) were particularly admired at IDHEC while Claire Denis was there. Everyone wanted to work with Eustache, she said, and Garrel was an idol because he was young (the same age as students at IDHEC), and he was able to make his own personal films. Denis reserves special praise for Jacques Rivette, who held a revered position at IDHEC. "No one had ever made a film like *Out One . . . Spectre* [1972], and where he ventured, no one has ventured since. He embodied the very spirit of freedom. My dream—my only dream at the time—was to meet Jacques Rivette" (Denorme and Douin 23). Denis graduated from IDHEC in 1972, and she not only met Rivette but also worked as his assistant and later, of course, directed the documentary about him.[1] Part of the reason Rivette asked Denis to direct the film is that he had directed the first film in the series, about Jean Renoir, and he had once been Renoir's assistant; therefore he thought it appropriate to ask a former assistant, whose work he admired, to direct the film about him.

Claire Denis's experience as an assistant director, which involved working with a number of different directors, lasted well over a decade. She began as an intern, then worked as a production assistant, a second assistant director, and a first assistant director. For the most part, Denis worked for directors who had independent visions of the cinema—Rivette, obviously, but also Dusan Makavejev (*Sweet Movie* [1974]) and Constantin Costa-Gavras (*Hanna K* [1983]). Eventually Denis worked with both Jim Jarmusch and Wim Wenders—with Jarmusch on *Down by Law* (1986), and with Wim Wenders on *Paris, Texas* (1984) and *Wings of Desire* (1987). While Denis obviously admires Wenders's and Jarmusch's films enormously, what she learned from them may have had more to do with strategies of financing and production, and clarity of vision, than with particular cinematic themes or styles: "I didn't have to work with them to learn about writing and directing films, I just had to be a spectator of their work" (Denorme and Douin 24). Wenders and Jarmusch were "solitary navigators," and from them she learned important rules for any independent director: self-reliance and tenacity.

So when Wenders invited Denis to work as his assistant, and in spite of the success and admiration she had garnered in this career, she already was planning her own future as a director. Interestingly, however, working as his assistant enabled Denis's commitment to making her own film. First, she was fascinated by the autonomy that Wenders had as a film director. "I sensed that he had put together a system of film production that seemed magical to me" (Denorme and Douin 24). Second, while traveling with Wenders throughout the U.S. West, she discovered her own cinematic territory. "During this trip across route 10 in the United States," says Denis, "we weren't just searching for locations. Wim Wenders was searching for his film. It was a moving experience for me to discover this landscape and to watch a man looking for himself. . . . I asked myself, Do I have a landscape? With Wim Wenders, I was travelling across the territory of cinema. But my own territory wasn't in the United States, or even in France (where I was born), but in certain countries in Africa. I knew I had to return to Africa to make *Chocolat*" (Truong 2003: 73–74).

Denis was still working as an assistant director when she began to work on the screenplay for *Chocolat* in 1985. She pursued funding opportunities relentlessly. When one looks at the credits for *Chocolat*, it is clear that she had learned an enormous amount about film production during what might be called her lengthy apprenticeship as an assistant—ten companies are listed, reflecting the history of the film's development (Gili 1988: 14). *Chocolat* also embodies what is one of the most distinctive aspects of Claire Denis's career: her consistent collaboration with Jean-Pôl Fargeau, with whom she has coauthored most of her films, and with Agnès Godard, on camera.

When *Chocolat* was released in 1988 (and was shown at the Cannes Film Festival that year), Claire Denis's career as an independent director was launched. While *Chocolat* had a lengthy gestation period, as most first features do, the amount of work that Claire Denis produced in the space of a few years—*Chocolat* came out in May of 1988, *Man No Run* in the fall of 1989, and *No Fear, No Die* and *Jacques Rivette, le veilleur* both appeared in 1990—is impressive.

In 1991, two short films appeared. In New York, Denis made *Keep It for Yourself*, a forty-minute film that was initially intended as a car commercial for Nissan. The film was part of a three-part feature called

Figaro Stories. Unfortunately *Keep It for Yourself* is not easy to see (it tends to be shown only at film festivals). It is a beautifully shot black and white film about a young French woman who comes to New York at the invitation of an American boyfriend who promptly disappears but leaves her the keys to his apartment. She ends up in a relationship with a man who breaks into her apartment to avoid the police. The film was produced by Good Machine, which has become a renowned producer of independent films; *Keep It for Yourself* was, in fact, their first film. The film was shot quickly, and it involved close collaboration with James Schamus, the producer, the filmmaker Sara Driver, who appears in the film, and the musician John Lurie. Agnès Godard was the cinematographer on the film, and black and white are used to maximum advantage to portray the city of New York. The film is scored by Lurie, who wrote the raucous "Breakfast Song" that provides the conclusion to the film. Finally, of course, the film is the first occasion where Denis and Vincent Gallo worked together, and he would go on to perform in three more of Denis's films.

Also in 1991, Denis directed another black and white film for the televised series *Ecrire contre l'oubli/Lest We Forget*, commissioned by Amnesty International. Individual filmmakers were paired with other artists in the making of the films, each of which focused on a particular political prisoner. Thirty filmmakers, including Chantal Akerman, Jean-Luc Godard, Patrice Leconte, Alain Resnais, Bertrand Tavernier, and Nadine Trintignant, made short films that were broadcast on French television from November 10 to December 10, 1991 (Voyeux 1991).

Pour Ushari Ahmed Mahmoud (Mahmoud was a political prisoner in Sudan) is a short film (four minutes) set to a haunting song by Alain Souchon, which was written for the occasion. Entitled "C'est déjà ça," the song is a mournful evocation of both political repression in Sudan and political exile in France. The film follows a young Sudanese man who walks, sometimes alone, sometimes accompanied by a friend, through the streets of Belleville in Paris. With tracking shots and a stunning use, again, of black and white, the film is a sad evocation of urban solitude. Yet the film is quite beautiful as well, particularly in terms of how visual encounters occur. The film is introduced with a title that reads: "In Paris, men dream." Obviously the Sudanese men who walk the streets, and who cross paths with another black man in a deserted market, are the dreamers of the film. But the film itself dreams of an encounter between the white singer and the black men. In the middle of the film, there is an interlude when we see Souchon singing in the studio. We see Souchon again at the conclusion of the film, sitting in a café, stirring his coffee, looking wistful. The two men whom we have been watching during the film walk by and seem to look into the café. Souchon looks up, and his gaze meets that of the other man whom we have seen in the market. The last shot of the film shows the young man as he enters the café, and as he appears to look at Souchon, he also appears to look at the viewer. The film imagines Paris, then, as a place where sidelong glances and chance encounters suggest limitation as well as possibility.

The following year, 1992, saw the release of *La Robe à cerceau/The Hoop Skirt* (a twenty-four-minute film), part of a series entitled "Monologues," in which, as the title of the series suggests, directors filmed dramatic monologues. The actor Jacques Nolot (who would later appear in both *J'ai pas sommeil* and *Nénette and Boni*) wrote the monologue. The film is shot in black and white, and it is relatively spare. First we see a woman (Dani) in a café, as she closes up for the night. In the background we hear the sound of a radio. The woman locks the door and makes one last cup of coffee for herself (with a bit of whiskey added). We then see, in a reverse shot, a man (Nolot) in the café, sitting at a table, with cigarettes, an ashtray, and a notebook. He appears to be waiting for the woman to finish her tasks before he begins to speak.

Most of the remainder of the film consists of the man reading aloud the story in his notebook: in the square of a small village, under an archway, there is a cobbler's shop. Inside the shop, two chairs support a coffin, and next to the coffin, a man sits in a chair and listens. A pregnant woman of about forty is counting, making preparations for the meal to follow the funeral the next day: there will be fourteen guests. Thus the monologue of Denis's film is the monologue of the woman as listened to by the man sitting in the chair, and as constructed and performed by Nolot, in the café, with the woman in the café, and us, as listeners. Throughout the telling of the story, we see reverse shots of the woman in the café, shots that show her both at closer and closer range and as more and more engaged and taken with the story. The cinematographer was Denis's usual collaborator, Agnès Godard, and the composition of each shot is a model of symmetry, with the two characters situated in different ways in their environment, framed by the space of the café, or in close-ups in which their bodies and their faces show their engagement with the story. Indeed, any connection between the man and the woman is constructed across and through the story. The "monologue" of the film, then, is situated constantly in the space of interactions across space and time.

These two films—*Pour Ushari Ahmed Mahmoud* and *The Hoop Skirt*—share an unusual quality, for they are perhaps the only films directed by Claire Denis that were not written by her (the "text" of *Pour Ushari Ahmed Mahmoud* is Souchon's song, and Nolot wrote the monologue for *La Robe à cerceau*). Central to both films, however, is the strong spirit of collaboration that inspires all of Denis's work.

The preparations for *J'ai pas sommeil,* which appeared at Cannes in 1994, were lengthy. Denis began work on another project before deciding that she was ready to tackle a subject as complex as the serial killer Thierry Paulin (the film was only "inspired" by the case, but it was received in France as resuscitating the case from the late 1980s). Denis was completing this film at the same time that she began shooting *U.S. Go Home,* her contribution to the enormously influential television series *Tous les garçons et les filles de leur âge.* In 1995, Denis contributed a short film to a British series entitled *Picture House*, in which filmmakers were asked to create short films (hers is two minutes long) inspired by works of art. Denis used a print from a collection entitled "Duo," by French artist Jacques Loustal (1994). Loustal's print shows a black man dressed in a white suit, who sits on a chair and observes the lower half of a white woman's body, stretched out on a bed. To the accompaniment of "Tin Tin Deo" (played by the Roy Nathanson Quartet), Denis's film moves from the print to an observer, played by Alex Descas, who is seen in close-up and extreme close-up as he smokes, apparently looks at the image (we don't see him and the image in the same shot), and stares into the camera. If Descas mirrors the man in the print, who would appear to be a prostitute's client, his gaze has considerably more range, particularly given that he looks directly at the camera, and at the spectator. The catalogue for the exhibition describes Denis's film as "a witty and erotic tension between voyeurism and black and white" ("Day of British Cinema" 1995).

U.S. Go Home finds a kind of sequel, as it were, in *Nénette and Boni,* which was released in 1996. While making preparations for *Nénette and Boni,* Denis was asked to contribute to the film *A Propos de Nice, la suite* (1995), which was intended as an homage to Jean Vigo and his 1930 film *A Propos de Nice.* Eight filmmakers contributed seven episodes to the film (one was codirected), and Denis's contribution features Grégoire Colin (the star of both *U.S. Go Home* and *Nénette and Boni*) in a ten-minute film, *Nice, Very Nice,* about a young man hired to kill a man who works in a street-food stand (Denis had read about the case, which took place in Nice, in the newspaper). Denis's major focus at the time was the preparation of *Nénette and Boni,* which was released in 1996.

Shortly after this release, Denis made a short film intended for an exhibition at the Cartier Foundation, *A Propos d'une déclaration.* Conceived as an homage to Nagisa Oshima's *In the Realm of Passion* (1978), the film became somewhat controversial but was projected at the foundation in 1997. Philippe Sollers curated an exhibition designed, initially, around the theme of "declarations of love" (later the exhibition was focused on "love," without the declarations). Denis was one of several filmmakers invited to make short films that would be shown continuously during the exhibit. Seen on its own terms, the film is a somewhat puzzling erotic fantasy. Alex Descas appears at the beginning of the film, first on a plane, then asleep in a room. A woman—we see her body, never her face—disrobes, gets into the bathtub, and proceeds to shave her pubic hair while a rubber duck looks on (as it were). When seen in context, the film is an interesting and witty response to Oshima's film, in which the male lover demands that his female lover shave her pubic hair. As Maureen Turim suggests, this possession of the woman in Oshima's film is a kind of writing on the body (1998: 150). The woman is ordered to shave by the man, but he is the one who performs the act. In Denis's film, the woman's body certainly is fragmented, but she is the one who initiates the shaving ritual.

Three feature films followed, one a year: *Beau travail* in 1999–2000, *Trouble Every Day* in 2001, and *Vendredi soir* in 2002. It is undoubtedly silly to try to impose any kind of "triptych" structure on these three films, but they do mark an interesting, if somewhat tenuous, inversion of the first three features. If *Chocolat, No Fear, No Die,* and *I Can't Sleep* are a kind a voyage—the first is "about colonization, the second about immigration, and the third about how people become assimilated to a society" (Benjamin 1995: 10), the three most recent films mark a movement away from the ways in which Africa inhabits the minds and bodies of those shaped by colonization, and toward, rather, the ways in which French (and, in the case of *Trouble Every Day,* American) identities are haunted by the spectre of former colonies that have become both images of another space and a kind of imaginary blank screen upon which to project white fears, fantasies, and desires. *Beau travail* is structured by an exiled legionnaire's reflections and memories of what happened in Djibouti, and *Trouble Every Day* traces a mysterious illness, associated with Guyana, that causes what might be called—very understatedly— sexual dysfunction. If *Vendredi soir* seems to have little to do with these evocations of former colonies, that is precisely the point: set completely in Paris, the film is a rarity in Claire Denis's career in that it features only white protagonists (of her other films, only *U.S. Go Home, Nénette and Boni,* and *La Robe à cerceau* feature predominantly white casts; the two male protagonists of *Beau travail* are white, but the cast of characters is extremely diverse). There are few white filmmakers about whom one can say that a particular film is unusual *because* it is about white people. Additionally, if we see these most recent three films together, another movement occurs in Denis's career, which is "toward Paris."

Another short film appeared in the fall of 2002, at about the same time as *Vendredi soir,* and it too is about movement, travel. *Vers Nancy/Towards Nancy* is a ten-minute film made for the televised series *Ten Minutes Older.* Fifteen filmmakers were invited to make ten-minute films about the passage of time. Denis's contribution is inspired by the philosopher Jean-Luc Nancy's book *L'Intrus* (2000), a study of "intrusion" in several senses of the term. *L'Intrus* is about strangerhood understood in cultural terms, but it is also about intrusion in a very personal sense. Nancy describes in his book the experience of undergoing a heart transplant, with attendant questions of identity, self, and, literally, grafting. *Towards Nancy* features Nancy playing himself. He is sitting in a train with a female student, herself a foreigner, and discussing "intrusion," what it means to be a "foreigner" and an "intruder." Their conversation cites a scene in Jean-Luc Godard's *La Chinoise* (1967), when Maoist student Véronique (Anne Wiazemsky) discusses revolution with the philosopher Francis Jeanson. Nancy's student wears the same kind of cap that Wiazemsky does in Godard's film, and *Towards Nancy* shows the pair framed by the train window, as in Godard's film (the sequence in *Towards Nancy* is also suggestive of Nana's conversation with philosopher Brice Parain in Godard's *My Life to Live* [1962]).

Towards Nancy cites Godard's films, but the conversation between teacher and student in Denis's film is interrupted by another kind of "intrusion." Their conversation concludes when Alex Descas, his black skin in heightened contrast (the film is shot in black and white) to their whiteness, enters their compartment and interrupts their philosophical conversation to ask when the train is due to arrive. The film ends, in other words, when an "intruder" comes into the train compartment—an intruder who brings the philosophical discussion to an abrupt halt, and whose black skin brings another kind of difference into the equation.

In terms of Denis's trajectory as an independent filmmaker, her work shares certain qualities with other filmmakers of her generation, but it is also unique. Denis certainly belongs to the tradition of auteur-ist cinema, a phrase that is unfortunately vague but which nonetheless applies to the consistently personal vision that she brings to her films. The auteurist tradition in French cinema is grounded in the New Wave, the loosely defined yet enormously influential development in French cinema from 1959 to the mid-1960s, that includes directors such as Godard and Rivette, as well as François Truffaut, Claude Chabrol, and Eric Rohmer. New Wave filmmakers, in their careers as critics (all of the directors mentioned above wrote about the cinema before they became filmmakers), promoted films that were part of the cinematic vision of a particular director, and as filmmakers, they developed in their own work a vision of the cinema as personal, intimate, and more open to the concrete experience of everyday life.

In a 1998 roundtable including Claire Denis, and organized by *Cahiers du Cinéma* for a special issue on the New Wave, Denis describes the intimacy and the new openness of filmmakers like Godard and Rivette; "The New Wave invited on board actors you'd want to meet in a café, or fall in love with" (Assayas 1998: 72). But she also stresses that New Wave filmmakers succeeded because of the way they situated themselves with respect to "money and film production" (Assayas 1998: 73). "Money and sex," summarizes Denis, "are what's important in defining the New Wave" (Assayas 1998: 74).

Auteurism has been criticized as a perspective that tends both to fetishize the director as a lone creator and to valorize formal innovation at the expense of all other concerns. In a way, auteurism has become such an ingrained notion in the understanding of film that it is impossible to dispense with it, but, of course, what matters is how the notion is used in the first place. Some filmmakers—many of them women—have been excluded from critical consideration because their work is not seen as measuring up to the standards of auteurism (needless to say, those standards are usually defined by male critics). And auteurism can place such an emphasis on the coherence of one artist's vision that significant changes and contradictions are ignored in the name of a single, overarching auteurist perspective.

Emma Wilson suggests that we use the notion of "personal history" not as a substitute for auteurism but as a useful reminder of what is at stake in the notion of a film author. As Wilson writes, "The director, and the other artists with whom he works, may seek to change the forms of representation and images produced, not for the sake of innovation alone, but in respect of the creative possibilities of a particular *histoire.* The director's perspective, the personal 'take' on the story, be it autobiographical or not, becomes of prime interest. . . . a director may seek to unravel or deconstruct an identity; be it artistic or personal, his own or a protagonist's" (1999: 19). Denis's own career is characterized less by "deconstructing" identities than by watching them take shape through individual bodies, relationships between bodies, and their movements across space. Yet Wilson's perspective is a useful corrective to the notion that auteurism is necessarily a totally useless and/or outdated concept (and as long as directors are classified as auteurs, particularly within certain national contexts, as Denis is, the concept of auteurism will remain with us).

In more general terms, Denis's career exemplifies multiple meanings of the notion of the auteur. Denis often reminds us, for instance, that to be an auteur is to be a self-promoter, to be constantly on the move for funding opportunities, to be aware of the cinema as a form of work as well as art (see Maule 1999). Auteurism, then, in the case of Claire Denis, provides both a cultural/historical framework for her work and an opportunity to see how her individual films form a whole—not a coherent whole, necessarily, but rather a set of preoccupations, desires, and concerns.

One of the paradoxes of film authorship, particularly in relationship to some of the greatest auteurs in French film history, like Jean Vigo and Jean Renoir, is that the supposedly "individual" vision of the director is made possible by collaboration, by working consistently with a group of other artists. There are few directors who better illustrate this apparent paradox than Claire Denis. Agnès Godard has been the cinematographer or assistant camera on nearly all of Denis's films (and they worked together when Denis was the assistant director on *Paris, Texas* and *Wings of Desire* as well). Jean-Pôl Fargeau (who is a successful playwright) has coauthored all of Denis's feature films, with the exception of *U.S. Go Home* (again, I am considering this one-hour film, coauthored by Denis and Anne Wiazemsky, as a feature) and *Vendredi soir* (Denis cowrote the film with Emmanuèle Bernheim, who wrote the novel upon which the film is based). Editor Nelly Quettier has worked on the last four of Denis's feature films. All of these collaborators have worked, of course, on other films as well, but they have not worked with any single director as consistently as they have with Denis. Denis and Fargeau clearly have established a partnership that works wonderfully, and Agnès Godard has a particular style that is ideal for Denis's films. When asked whether her consistent collaboration with Denis risked become too routine, Godard replied: "We started out at the same time. Between us there is a complicity and a strange passionate relationship, an intimacy that is centered on the cinema" (Audé and Tobin 2000: 133).

Denis's spirit of collaboration includes music, too. Abdullah Ibrahim wrote the original music for both *Chocolat* and *No Fear, No Die*. The Tindersticks have scored two of Denis's films, *Nénette and Boni* and *Trouble Every Day* (and they were deeply involved in the conceptualization of the film; they did not simply create a soundtrack after the fact), and Dickon Hinchcliffe (a member of Tindersticks) wrote the music for *Friday Night*. In all of these cases, Denis worked with the musicians as the film was being conceptualized and produced. About her approach to music in her films, Denis is clear: "What's called the film score, that intervention after-the-fact . . . is often a way to impose 'character psychology' (which horrifies me), and it is completely contrary to my idea of the cinema" (Jousse 2002: part 2). Interestingly, the collaboration with musicians has worked both ways; Denis notes that the Tindersticks told her that working with her on the music for *Nénette and Boni* gave them the opportunity to think through and conceptualize their next album (Jousse 2002: part 2). Indeed, at virtually all stages of collaboration—from the concept of a film, to the screenplay, to the thinking through of various aspects of the final film—Denis is actively and passionately involved with her coworkers.

One of the most striking aspects of Denis's collaborative approach to filmmaking is the relationship she develops with actors. Denis has worked with particular actors many times over. Isaach de Bankolé, who stars as Protée in *Chocolat,* also stars in *No Fear, No Die.* Alex Descas appears in *No Fear, No Die, J'ai pas sommeil, Nénette and Boni,* and *Trouble Every Day,* as well as in *A Propos d'une declaration* and *Duo.* Alice Houri and Grégoire Colin star in *U.S. Go Home* and *Nénette and Boni.* Colin appears again in *Beau travail,* as well as in *Nice, Very Nice.* Vincent Gallo appears in *Keep It for Yourself, Nénette and Boni,* and *Trouble Every Day.* Béatrice Dalle is featured in *J'ai pas sommeil* and *Trouble Every Day.* Many of the actors with whom Denis works make small, almost cameo appearances in her films; thus Colin appears briefly in *Vendredi soir,* Alice Houri in *J'ai pas sommeil,* Solveig Dommartin (the female lead in *S'en Fout la mort*) in *J'ai pas sommeil.* Richard Courcet, who was not a professional actor when Denis cast him as Camille in *J'ai pas sommeil,* makes a brief appearance in *Nénette and Boni* and has a supporting role in *Beau travail.*

Denis has appeared on various French television programs with actors from her films, and the unique relationship she has with them is palpable. The temptation is to say that the relationship is "like" something else, but most metaphors are inadequate (Claire Denis does not appear to be—to take the typical adjectives applied to women—motherly, for example, or flirtatious with her stars). There appears to be genuine fondness, but there is professionalism as well; actors and director show respect and admiration for each other. A special alchemy connects Denis with her actors and affirms her particular view that what matters, in films, are the people—the bodies, the characters, the actors—that populate them. When *I Can't Sleep* was released, Denis responded to an interviewer's comment about how, in the film, the portrayal of bodies attains a fullness, a density: "I'm not saying this as a joke: capturing bodies on film is the only thing that interests me" (Jousse and Strauss 1994: 25). This may sound like a bit of an overstatement, but at the same time it makes sense, for all of the qualities that characterize Denis's approach to the cinema—wandering through space, curiosity, vagabondage—center, sooner or later, on a fascination with the human body.

Of course, a fascination with the body does not necessarily translate into a particularly close relationship with actors. In Denis's case, the very process of putting bodies on screen is, simultaneously, a process of discovery along with the actors, not an imposition of one particular vantage point. "A film is an expandable structure," says Denis, "where space is invaded by the actors. So everything is possible" (Ancian 2002: 6). Shortly after the appearance of *Chocolat*, Denis articulated the particular relationship she enjoys with actors in a way that applies to all of her films: "I loved the actors [in *Chocolat*], and they gave me a sense of fulfillment. This particular relationship, between director and actor, is neither admiration nor friendship, and it certainly is not seduction. It is pure love, a kind of energy . . ." (Bonvoisin and Brault-Wiart 1989: 43). Several years later, Denis used a word to describe her ideal actor that is particularly fitting: a companion. "Even today," she said, "it's hard for me to work with actors who are not companions" (Assayas et al. 1998: 72). Denis is clear that she is captivated by her actors. "Sometimes, when I go to the cinema," she said in 1999, "I'm so fascinated by a particular actor or actress that I have only one desire, and that's to write for them and work with them" (Vallaeys 1999: 16).

Claire Denis's position as an independent director is complicated, one would assume, by two factors. First, she is a woman in a world that remains predominantly male; and second, she is a white woman who makes films about black people, and more often than not, black men. I have already suggested that as a woman director, Denis confounds expectations. A televised report on the opening days of *Trouble Every Day* featured prominently the response of a (male) spectator to the film: How could a woman have made that? Denis watched the man's reactions on a monitor and then replied: "People who say, 'Why do women make films like this?' still think that women don't have vast territories to explore" ("Report on *Trouble Every Day*").

In an interesting interview with director Catherine Breillat, on the occasion of the release of Breillat's very controversial film *Romance* in 1999, Denis referred to a comment Breillat had made about how Breillat's filmmaking leans toward women, and Denis's, toward men. Denis says: "You said I was 'lying in wait' among men, and I think that's true, I'm someone who 'lies in wait,' whereas you make things happen. . . . I often feel the presence of the director—not only in my own films—as someone who is 'lying in wait,' without any intention of making something happen. The author is there to see where the characters are going to take the film. But in your case, I think you are there to make something happen with your characters" (Breillat and Denis 1999: 42). The distinction between "lying in wait" and "making something happen" seems to displace Breillat's commentary about gender, and the notion of "lying in wait" can suggest a certain passivity of the film director that seems inaccurate. But Denis's larger point suggests that if she is, indeed, a "woman director," it is not because of her subject matter but because of her style.

When *Chocolat* came out in 1988, its quasi-autobiographical format and its frame story—the adult France who returns to Cameroon—made it seem as though Denis was a director whose work would soon be discussed within the context of female authorship and feminist aesthetics. Women and female points of view are important in Denis's films, but not in the way one might expect. True, Daïga's arrival in Paris and her discovery of Camille's crimes provide a narrative structure for *J'ai pas sommeil,* and in some sense her view provides a privileged frame for the story. But Denis's films are more about men than they are about women. While I think that Denis's approach to gender is innovative, sometimes troubling (as in *Trouble Every Day*), and always provocative, there is no question that her films both suggest and close down the possibilities of distinctly female points of view. Denis's most consistent collaborators are both women (Godard, Quettier) and men (Fargeau); she works equally well with male and female actors. Even when women occupy small roles in Denis's films, they are crucially important. *Beau travail,* for instance, is generally described as a film about men, about masculinity, and this is, of course, accurate; but the female figures in the film function as a kind of chorus—again, not unlike Denis herself—observing and commenting upon the follies of men.

Denis is characteristically ambivalent when she describes herself as a woman director, and this is not surprising, since she is an artist who thrives on ambiguity. Sometimes her comments sound like a celebration of some mystical female essence ("cinema is a physical medium, and women are more aware of it" [Colpin 1997: 1]). Denis has claimed that being a woman has not posed any particular problems for her in her career ("I never felt the problem of being a woman director. There was no special difficulty. If I don't make a film one year, it's because of me and not because I'm a woman and I don't get all I need" [Jones 1992: 14]). At the same time, in interviews Denis sometimes subtly, but forcefully, makes an observation that punctures sexist pretensions. Describing *Beau travail,* Denis speaks of the ruse of making men believe that a masculine, virile world is one of harmony, while all other worlds—especially feminine ones—are chaotic (Denorme and Douin 26). In the same interview, in response to a comment about Denis's attraction to the margin, to solitary men, she replies: "And solitary women" (Denorme and Douin 26).

Any reluctance on Denis's part to classify herself as a "woman director" is also a reflection of the particular status of women filmmakers in France. In the introduction to *Cinema and the Second Sex,* a study of women filmmakers in France in the 1980s and 1990s, Carrie Tarr and Brigitte Rollet note the paradox of women directors in France. "It is not surprising that French women directors routinely reject the label of 'woman director,'" they note, "since claiming a supposedly gender-neutral auteur status is often the best way to gain legitimacy and recognition within the film industry." Yet at the same time, "an acceptance of auteurism has enabled women to impose themselves as directors to an extent which is unique to France" (2001: 10–11).

While Denis may be reluctant about the relationship between gender and authorship, she has associated spectatorship with women, and even though this is an indirect connection (as many connections tend to be in Claire Denis's work), she echoes many arguments that have been made in feminist film theory over the years about the contradictory identities embodied by women in relationship to the cinema. An interviewer noted that in *No Fear, No Die,* women were largely absent, and that the character of Toni (played by Solveig Dommartin) is an archetype of the unavailable, desirable woman. Denis agrees but adds: "The friendship between the two men is quickly perceived by a woman. I think that we women are good witnesses; in looking, in seeing, we find pleasure. Looking at what is outside of me pleases me enormously" (Heyman 1990).

Denis's status as a white director, whose own personal history was shaped by colonization and decolonization, is equally ambiguous. As I note above, there are very few white directors about whom one can say that a film is exceptional because it features an all-white cast. Denis's world is diverse, but it would be too easy to say that Denis, unlike many contemporary directors, is simply portraying the reality of a "French" culture that is hybrid, multiple, and multiracial. This is true, but Denis is drawn to the representation of black men (and, less so, black women). This does not necessarily mean that she fetishizes black men in the same way that white directors often fetishize blacks or that male directors fetishize women. Yet because Denis's own desires as a filmmaker entail questions concerning race and racial boundaries, her work is inevitably seen in relationship to cultural anxieties about the relationship between white people and black people. In response to an interviewer's comment that her male actors seem to function as muses, Denis replied, speaking particularly of Alex Descas: "Alex is a muse, it's true. He's a muse because he always was a sort of mirror for me. Something in his look always reflected something in which I was interested. . . . I knew immediately he was not really a stranger to me, he was like a sort of companion or, not a brother I would say, but he would help me to understand more" (Hart 2003: 5). One could find the very notion of a black actor functioning as a "muse" perturbing, but Claire Denis problematizes and makes visible her own fascinations and desires, while refusing to bow to any simplistic notions of what might or might not be considered acceptable. Sometimes her films take on, very deliberately, the difficult intersections of race and gender, as in *No Fear, No Die* and *J'ai pas sommeil.* In both cases, Denis had to deal with accusations of political incorrectness, between the black man who dies, in the former film, and the black (as well as gay and HIV-positive) serial killer in the latter.

At other times, one senses that Denis practices not "color-blind" casting but casting attentive to assumptions that viewers often make about what are "appropriate" roles for black actors. Hence Alex Descas plays a physician in *Nénette and Boni,* a role that "could" have been played by a white man. Similarly, interracial relationships are presented without need of further explanation in Denis's films; in both *J'ai pas sommeil* and *Trouble Every Day*, Béatrice Dalle and Alex Descas play a married couple. And sometimes, racial and ethnic identity are simply not addressed; in *Nénette and Boni,* for example, both Grégoire Colin and Alice Houri "could" be North African, as could their father, played by Jacques Nolot.

But more important than the controversies that Denis's films sometimes inspire, or the matter-of-fact way in which a racially diverse world is created in her films, is the fact that bodies, and black male bodies in particular, *are* examined and observed in Denis's films. Along with voyeurism, fetishism has been seen as one of the founding principles of male visual pleasure. Denis's films suggest, rather, that the pleasures of seeing in the cinema belong to women as both directors and spectators. Claiming these pleasures for women is one thing; it is not quite the same thing to claim these pleasures for white spectators and directors in terms of black bodies. I am not going to suggest the easy way out by claiming that Denis's cinema is anti-fetishistic or anti-voyeuristic. I do suggest that the ways in which gender and race are addressed in her films can never be defined in terms of any one particular concept of what the cinema is, what it "should" be, or what it might be in terms of ways of seeing through the lenses of gender, race, and nation.

One of the central preoccupations of Denis's work is a sense of displacement, of choosing to move around an object or a theme or a person, instead of moving in directly. Denis has described her 1994 film *J'ai pas sommeil* as structured by *le jeu de l'oie,* the "goose game," in which one moves in a circular direction on the game board from the outside to the center. Thus the spectator's journey in the film follows that of Daïga, a Lithuanian immigrant who is driving into Paris in order to make a new life for herself, and her discoveries are those of the film's viewers. *Nénette and Boni* (1996) opens with a scene in which a hustler attempts to sell counterfeit long-distance telephone cards to a group of African immigrants. The hustler has no direct relationship to the central plot or characters of the film, yet the phone cards pop up at various moments in the film, a reminder of both the complexities of "communication" and the off-center moments that are as central to Denis's films as they are to the experience of contemporary life. Denis's films are populated by vagabonds of various kinds, male and female, black and white, who move around and through the various boundaries that shape human existence.

The sense of vagabondage, of moving around rather than directly toward an object, describes Claire Denis's career as well as her films. As an independent filmmaker who has had to learn virtually everything there is to learn about funding, Claire Denis remains stubbornly and admirably true to her own vision about what matters and about what is important. Part of that process is seizing opportunities when they arise and make artistic and cinematic sense.

In 1997, Denis was one of sixty-six filmmakers involved in the support of the *sans-papiers,* or illegal immigrants, whose status and livelihood in France were threatened by new anti-immigration laws. Phil Powrie sees the political activism of these filmmakers as marking a new stage in the relationship between cinema and politics, particularly in terms of what has been called a "new realism" in French cinema (1999: 10–18). In the case of Claire Denis, the involvement in the support of the *sans-papiers* seems more important as an indication of her commitment to political principles than as a motivation to make a different kind of cinematic work. Denis has said that her experience with the mobilization on behalf of immigrants was instrumental in how she thought about Jean-Luc Nancy's work *L'Intrus* in relationship to the film *Vers Nancy.* But she resists the notion of any kind of political "message" in her work. "Films are always political, whether we want them to be or not" says Denis (Jousse 2002: part 4). This suggests that she is less interested in making films with a particular political perspective than in making films that explore the very possibility of a range of (cinematic) perspectives.

A scene that Claire Denis decided not to shoot in *Beau travail* suggests that perhaps it is more appropriate to think of the political dimensions of her work in terms of ethics. Near the beginning of the film, we see the passing landscape of Djibouti from the inside of a train, populated by local men and women. According to Denis, that sequence was inspired by a young woman who lived in a nearby town, a refugee from Eritrea, one of many young girls who took up arms during the war. As their train passed in the desert, Denis and her crew often saw the young woman dressed in combat fatigues, her head shaved, carrying her Kalashnikov, and sometimes they saw her in town. Denis's intention was to include a character based on the young girl in the train scene. But ultimately, Denis decided not to shoot the scene. Once the film was over, Denis and her crew would leave the country, and she thought it would be difficult for a young woman to shave her head and appear in the film, particularly given that refugees could be singled out for discrimination. Perhaps the presence of this figure would have added an explicit political dimension to the film, but as Denis points out, there is always something political that occurs when one sets up a camera and films. Denis points to the way in which Gilles Sentain is revived—resurrected—by the Djiboutians, and describes this act of salvation as something that isn't a "message—it is work that is far better than a message" (Renouard and Wajeman 2001: 10–11).

In a different context, Denis is known as a director who forges bonds with other directors. In a 1997 profile on Denis, Jean-Michel Frodon wrote: "Perhaps this sense of sharing explains something particular about Claire Denis: she is friendly—something uncommon in this world—with other filmmakers. There are Rivette and Wenders, there is Léos Carax, Sharunas Bartas, Olivier Assayas and many others" (1997: 17). Denis responded to Frodon: "Often friendship develops because I liked a film, or someone liked one of mine. When you feel doubt about a project, it's necessary to be able to share it with other filmmakers. Other people's films stimulate ours, a beautiful shot makes you want to make a film, not in order to imitate what you've seen but because it's a source of desire and energy" (Frodon 1997: 17).

Some of the specific forms this solidarity with other filmmakers has taken include cowriting with Yousry Nasrallah the film *El Medina* (2000) (the two also collaborated on a film about singer Jean-Louis Murat, which was never completed). Denis has also appeared in the works of other directors. Laetitia Masson's 1995 feature *En avoir (ou pas)* tells the story of Alice (Sandrine Kiberlain), a young woman fired from her factory job, who decides to make a new life elsewhere. Relatively early in the film, Alice meets her mother in a park, at a low-rent housing development. The mother, played by Denis, is a small blonde woman with a husky voice, who is taking care of a neighbor's children. The mother and daughter sit together on a bench, and Alice berates her mother for how much she smokes. Given that Laetitia Masson is of a younger generation of French women filmmakers, it is tempting to see Denis's role in the film as figuratively as well as literally maternal. Denis said of Masson that "she was one of the first of the young film-makers to write to me saying they liked what I did. Laetitia told me that she thought of me as her 'godmother,' which was very touching. Noémie Lvovsky, too, considers me like an elder sister. But do I feel close to them? Yes and no. That's to say I'm touched by their comments but I don't like all their films" (Darke 2000: 18).

Familiar and traditional categories of female identity do not really apply to Claire Denis as a filmmaker, and in the rare appearances she has made in the films of other people, her presence signals, rather, solidarity with a community of filmmakers (even when she doesn't "like all their films"). Denis makes a cameo appearance in *Vénus beauté (institut),* Tonie Marshall's 1999 film, as an asthmatic client who is afraid of receiving a treatment. Claire Denis's films are very different from Tonie Marshall's, yet there is clearly a relationship of respect between the two women, whose directing careers began at approximately the same time (Tonie Marshall was an actress who directed her first film, *Pentimento,* in 1989).

I've described Denis's cinema as attentive to the margins and to the periphery, and as discussed earlier, this includes marginalized people and groups. The problem with such a view is that for there to be a sense of the margin or the periphery, there needs to be a sense of the "center." Denis has said that "you can only feel yourself an outsider if you are part of a community. The outsider's view, I don't believe in it" (Ancian 2002: 3). The Têtes Brûlées may well be outsiders in France, but constantly they refer their perceptions of the country to what they know from French colonization and encounters with white people. Yet being part of a community means having shifting relationships to it, and Denis's cinema is attentive to those shifts.

Denis's focus on margins and the periphery also involves attentiveness to details that can escape our attention in everyday situations, and in this sense, too, there is always a sense of discovery in her films. In the DVD commentary for *Friday Night,* Denis describes the extensive preparations and restrictions that were necessary to be able to film on Paris streets at night: they couldn't shoot until after 10:00 P.M., they couldn't make any noise, and the placement of the cars had to be determined down to the last detail. Denis says that when you make a film, you prepare every detail ahead of time, you plan and you set up and you make sure everything is perfect, and then, when the shooting actually occurs, it is like flying a trapeze with no net. There is always a detail that can come along and threaten to upset everything that has been planned. Denis points to the dog in the Lumière brothers' film *Workers Leaving the Factory* (1895); the film was obviously prepared with great care, but when the little dog pops into the frame, you sense that it was a chance happening. It comes as no surprise that Denis loves those little details, the things that aren't planned (Denis and Jones 2003). One always has the sensation, in Denis's film, of paying attention to just those details.

In 1995, Claire Denis was one of the filmmakers who was asked, on the occasion of a television program about a conference on the "first century" of the cinema, why she makes films and for whom. Denis responded by citing an anecdote from her work as an assistant director on Jim Jarmusch's film *Down by Law* (1986). The crew received permission to film inside a prison in New Orleans, and she was surprised to learn that they would have virtually no restrictions. Except for one: They were not permitted to have any eye contact with the prisoners. "I thought the phrase—'no eye contact'—was funny but sad at the same time, because we were making a film, and that's exactly what making a film is about—the desire for eye contact. Encountering a look that is going to cross yours, in that moment when you establish contact, there might be a hesitation, but at the same time it's a very strong sensation. . . . The desire to make a film is the desire to see others" (*Le Cinéma vers son second siècle*). Seeing others may well be what the cinema is all about. In the films of Claire Denis, the process of seeing and the conceptualization of those "others" create works that inspire, that move, and that suggest the vitality of the cinema.

Border Patrols: *Chocolat* and *No Fear, No Die*

Claire Denis's first feature film, *Chocolat* (1988), tells a story in flashback. The time is the present or the not-too-distant past, and a French woman, France, who appears to be in her thirties, has returned to Cameroon, the country where she grew up. Through the majority of the film we see France as a child, in the late 1950s. France is the child of a colonial official and his wife, and France's most significant interactions are with the family servant, or "boy," Protée.[2] Given that Claire Denis grew up in Cameroon during a period of time that coincides with the flashback of the film, the connections with the director's own personal history are apparent. In sharp contrast, Denis's second feature, *No Fear, No Die* (1990), is set in contemporary Rungis, on the outskirts of Paris, and it is a story about two men, both black and both immigrants (most likely illegal), who train birds for cockfighting. Any traces of the autobiographical seem to have vanished. But *Chocolat* may well be a more interesting film for what it suggests about the powers of observation than for the story it tells about a white girl growing up in Africa. In that sense, Claire Denis's first two fictional films have more in common than what might first appear to be the case, for they are connected by an exploration of how various borders—those of time and of race and gender—are approached, contemplated, and, sometimes, crossed.

Denis encountered many difficulties, particularly financial, in the making of *Chocolat*. The film went through many changes in personnel, and at various points in the production it was unclear whether the film would be completed or not (Bonvoisin and Brault-Wiart 1989). For Denis herself, the film changed contours. Initially, Denis was considering making a film about African American GIs who moved to Africa after the war in Vietnam, but eventually she discarded the idea (Chutkow 1989: 29). She also struggled with the question of point of view, and Denis has always resisted overly simplistic readings of the film as pure autobiography. "Truthfully," she said, the film "isn't really that connected to my own personal experience, it is really more of a collection of received ideas . . . it is more a large-scale collective story of the colonizers than the individual story of a white girl and a 'boy'" (Gili 1988: 15).

Thus *Chocolat* is not only an exploration of a white child's upbringing in former French colony Cameroon, but it is also a reflection on the ways in which French colonial identity leaves its marks on those who travel in its wake—filmmakers and audiences as well as fictional characters. The film follows the journey of France, who returns to Cameroon as an adult. We first see her on the beach, observing a black man and his son as they frolic in the waves. Little information is given about any of these characters, so that viewers might well assume that the father and son are African and that France is, as the black man later assumes, a tourist. In fact the man is an African American expatriate to Africa (and hence evokes one of Denis's original ideas for the film), while France grew up in Cameroon. Appearances are deceiving, but more important, the very claim to the visibility and transparency of African identity is put into question from the outset of the film.

The man offers France a ride, and the movement of the car along the African road gives way to the extended flashback that constitutes most of the film. France Dalens as a young child lives in a colonial outpost, with her mother, Aimée, and her father, Marc, a colonial officer. France's life centers around Protée, the family servant, or "boy," who functions as both a mother and a father to the child. France is a part of what Stuart Hall calls the "colonial family romance," that is, the French family and the servants who negotiate virtually every aspect of their lives (Hall 1992: 49). France's closest companion is Protée. Their relationship shows genuine affection, yet at the same time France seems to be learning her colonial role quite well. At one point in the film, for instance, Protée waits on France who is seated alone at the dinner table, and she orders him to taste her soup, in a gesture that is both intimate and authoritarian.

Denis has acknowledged that *Chocolat* was partially inspired by Cameroonian author Ferdinand Oyono's novel *Une vie de boy.* Oyono's novel tells the story of a young Cameroonian man, Toundi, who becomes a house servant—a boy—and through his own position within the household comes to understand the arbitrariness of the power of the white colonials. The colonials in the novel are foolish and hypocritical. The novel has become a classic of African literature written in French. Here, the power structure of colonialism is turned inside out, with white people functioning as objects of curiosity. The novel is written as the found journals of Toundi, who is—like Protée—a house servant for a colonial administrator. Originally published in 1956, *Une vie de boy* has been described by Denis as a book that marked her adolescence, and *Chocolat,* she has said, is "a bit like the memory of that book" (Festival du vent 1998). The parallels are obvious, insofar as the similar positions of Toundi and Protée are concerned, for both are servants upon whom the household depends absolutely but who are expected to be invisible when the situation demands. Richard Bjornson's description of *Une vie de boy* is applicable to *Chocolat* as well: the Europeans "want to regard the houseboy as a 'thing that obeys,' but his potential for unmasking their pretensions makes them fear that he is actually a 'person who sees'" (1991: 79).

The memory of Oyono's novel may function in other ways in Denis's film as well. The novel is structured as the recollections of a man who finds Toundi's journals after his death, so there is a frame narrative in the novel that may have inspired Denis's use of the extended flashback in *Chocolat*. The frame narrative gives the events of the film a sense of recollection, of a childhood that is mourned, certainly, but also set in a very distant, irretrievable past. The intimacy between France and Protée is forever lost, and the structure of the film prevents the flashback section from being seen as a glorious past.

Yet there is a striking difference between the novel and the film in terms of the frame story. The "found" journals of Toundi are first-person accounts, so even while the immediacy of the journals is mediated through their discovery by someone else, there is still the creation of a subjective narrator. In sharp contrast, Denis resolutely avoided any attempt to create an African perspective or point of view in the film. "The experience of whites is always the same," said Denis. "We approach, approach, approach, but we never quite reach the heart of Africa. In *Chocolat,* I always tried to maintain only the perspective of the whites. I just didn't think I should pretend to understand the black point of view" (Chutkow 1989: 29). This may explain why, for example, there is virtually nothing in the film to give us a sense of Protée's identity outside of his work. He is seen only very briefly with a female companion early on, who virtually disappears from the film. Indeed, Denis says that while she and Fargeau were writing the screenplay, they insisted that there would be no scenes of the African domestic workers interacting among themselves. "I told myself," said Denis, "that if I mixed their words into the communication void between white people, it would be nothing more than 'musical' and 'decorative'" (Strauss 1990: 33).

Denis's resolute refusal to attempt to create anything but a white point of view might be admirable, since she insists that she cannot have access to a perspective that is not hers. Yet Denis's assessment of a white perspective can seem a bit defensive, as in these remarks on the film:

> When I was making *Chocolat* I think that I had a desire to express a certain guilt I felt as a child raised in a colonial world. When the film

was completed I was asked to write a piece on it for the press booklet. Unsure of what to write, I found an introduction to an anthology of Black literature and poetry by Jean-Paul Sartre which suggested that for three thousand years the official view of the world had been a white view and he now welcomed an alternative—the view from those who had been watched, what they saw when they looked at us, the white Europeans. I put this in the booklet because I thought that there was very little else I could say: knowing I was white, I tried to be honest in admitting that *Chocolat* is essentially a white view of the "other." (Denis in Petrie 1992: 66–67)

Denis made this statement at a filmmakers' panel following a discussion of her film in the context of contemporary European cinema. At this event, *Chocolat* was criticized for being, in the end, a Eurocentric film, because its emphasis was on the powerlessness of France to confront both its and her colonial past (see Ang 1992).

While I do not agree with this reading of the film, I believe it is suggestive of the potential double bind of a film like *Chocolat*. In acknowledging the dependence of white colonials on black Africans, the film offers a critique. But it also is more than a critique; it is a poetic exploration of how the differences between whites and blacks can be seen differently, beyond the clichés of the colonial encounter. Colonialism may always be there, on the horizon—which, as Marc explains to the child France, is a line that is visible and invisible at the same time. When Denis "admits" that *Chocolat* is "essentially a white view of the 'other'" (Denis in Petrie 1992: 67), it sounds a bit defeatist, as if white perspectives are always the same, and whether romanticizing or condescending toward Africa, always essentially racist. France's "powerlessness" seems to me much less important than the relationships of vision—between France and Mungo Park in the present and France and Protée in the past, but also between the camera and the scene, and the spectator and the screen.

The question of point of view in *Chocolat* is complex and tends to refer more to a generalized perspective, whether in ideological or narrative terms. Occasionally the flashback section of the film is referred to as the girl's point of view, given that her relationship with Protée is central to the film. This is a bit misleading: literally, because the girl is not present at everything that the spectator sees; and figuratively, because point of view in film is rarely defined in terms of a single character; it is, rather, the way in which the spectator's view is shaped and defined across a range of perspectives. Hence, while France's friendship with Protée is the thread that runs throughout the flashback section of the film, the major intrigue is developed through the arrival of different people at the Dalens home.

Marc is often away, and during one of his absences, a man named Jonathan Boothby arrives and flirts with Aimée. Later, when Marc is at home, a dramatic event brings the various facets of colonial identity into focus. A plane is forced to land, bringing a group of people who embody colonial clichés: a new colonial officer and his wife (when the wife falls ill, they are horrified at the thought of being treated by an African doctor); a cynical and overtly racist trader who travels with an African mistress kept out of sight; a former seminary student who flouts colonial conventions (he showers where the black servants shower) without questioning his own arrogance (he provokes Protée, presumably because Protée is a docile servant). The plane cannot leave until it is repaired, so the visit is a prolonged one. If the first part of the extended flashback of the film contrasts Marc's travels as a colonial officer with life at the Dalens home while he is gone, the arrival of the plane sets up a series of confrontations at the homesite. This group provides both a gamut of stereotypes of the relationship between white people and colonialism and a framework within which to see the interactions between Protée and the little girl, as well as Protée and the white family in general, Aimée in particular.

Luc, the former seminary student, is perhaps the most obvious catalyst of the drama that ensues. He mocks Protée mercilessly for his obedience and his docility. While Luc seems to have convinced himself that he is a radical who challenges the colonial order, his humiliation of Protée differs little from the manifestations of the overt racism of the coffee planter. The band of colonial stereotypes that invade the Dalens home offers extreme examples of the interaction between whites and blacks, to which the behavior of the Dalens family is contrasted but also compared. The contrast is apparent when a Cameroonian man, obviously held in high respect, brings an animal to the Dalens family. He is treated kindly and gratefully by Aimée, while the coffee planter insists on transportation out of the area and is generally rude and obnoxious. The contrast is again apparent when the African doctor comes to treat the newly arrived French woman; he is friendly with the Dalens family but is repudiated by the couple, for neither of them can bear the idea of being treated by an African doctor. Yet the contrast can be deceiving, for the new colonial officers may, perhaps, mirror the Dalens family when they arrived. And more important, however benevolent Marc and Aimée may seem in comparison to the others, they are still agents of colonial rule.

In any case, there is a continuum between the plane's occupants and the Dalens family, and it is established most forcefully through Aimée. After Protée has a violent confrontation with Luc, Protée sends Luc away, exercising his role as protector of the house. When Protée enters the house, Aimée makes a move toward sexual contact. Aimée takes hold of Protée's calf, and he steps away from her, uttering "*non.*" Protée is quickly dispatched from the house to the grounds as obvious punishment for humiliating the mistress of the house. This is not the first sign we have seen of an erotic connection between the two, insofar as Aimée is concerned; earlier in the film (during the visit by Jonathan Boothby), Aimée asks Protée to help her dress. Interestingly, Aimée's actual move toward physical contact with Protée occurs not while her husband is away on one of his trips, but rather while he is present in the house. It is as if Aimée's attraction to Protée is shaped by the visibility of colonial clichés.

Where *Chocolat* departs from those clichés is in its refusal to grant the fulfillment of the sexual wish. One of Denis's arguments with her producers had to do precisely with this point; they wanted there to be sexual contact, while Denis insisted that it not take place. One of the posters for the film reads as a kind of symptom of the function of sexual contact in the film; we see Aimée in a large close-up against the background of Africa, as if this were a film centered on her (obviously she is a central character, but this is still somewhat deceptive advertising!). By refusing to fulfill Aimée's wish, the film focuses attention, rather, on what that sexual desire signifies for white women in colonized Africa. A telling moment in this regard occurs when a group of colonial wives sit together, as the runway is being built for the departure of the airplane, and talk about how handsome Protée is. Their objectification of black men is obvious, but it also speaks to one of the key elements of virtually all of Denis's work: objectification is one of the ways in which people engage with their own situations, and for white women who function as wives and mothers in contexts that are isolating, fantasies about African men are one of the ways in which they attempt to create a world of their own.

Protée and the little girl become forever estranged after the thwarted sexual encounter. When France goes to visit Protée after his banishment to the garage, he tells her that a pipe is not at all hot to the touch, and to prove it, he grasps the pipe. Following his example, France takes hold of the pipe but is shocked to discover that it is hot enough to burn her skin. Protée repudiates France, and in the process marks the little girl's flesh as well as his own. The scene is heavily symbolic, for at the conclusion of this narrative, Protée repudiates both the nation and the girl. The setting of the flashback section of the film, in the late 1950s, thus traces not only a child's colonial upbringing but also the desire for independence from the colonial family and colonial rule—on the part of Cameroonians themselves, as embodied by Protée.

Most commentaries on *Chocolat* focus on the story of France's childhood, which does indeed take up the majority of the film. But the frame story makes clear that the extended flashback is a function of memory and a desire to situate one's self in relationship to Africa. As I have noted, Denis was aware of the dangers of making a film about white people in Africa. Part of the rationale for the frame narrative of the film was to make clear that for white people, especially those who have lived in Africa, any recollection of Africa is shaped and formed by very particular circumstances. This may seem to be an obvious comment in an era of postcolonial awareness and theorization of the many ways in which whiteness and its attendant privileges impose visions and stories on the rest of the world. But in *Chocolat,* the function of whiteness, as both a political/cultural privilege and as a fact of life, is a visual/narrative fact as well as a political one. In other words, the film emphasizes and draws attention to the status of white observation not by talking about it but by making it an integral part of the film. By making the film a story about a white woman's attempt to reconnect with her past, the film evokes memory, to be sure, but it also explores the nature of seeing and being seen, of listening and silence.

One of the most interesting commentaries on the film appeared in the French newspaper *Libération,* and it has been cited numerous times by Denis as an astute articulation of precisely what *Chocolat* stakes as its territory. Paul Jorion's "Dans le ventre de la nounou cosmique" (In the Womb of the Cosmic Wet Nurse) takes *Chocolat* as an exploration of what becomes of white identity in Africa. Noting that some have criticized the film for its caricatural cast of characters, Jorion notes that this is precisely what white people become in Africa, caricatures of themselves, fearful and "pathetically dependent" upon Africans who become nursemaids, whether they are "boys" (like Protée), cooks, or servants (1988: 9). "Black Africa," concludes Jorion, "slowly invades the European like a precious tumor, a Truth about ourselves slowly hollowing out its place, a truth otherwise lost in the painful emergence from childhood" (1988: 9). Thus France may well be returning to Africa to discover not a place or a presence but an absence. The "Truth" of which Jorion speaks is particularly accented in white children, whose light skin and hair "is a provocation to the nasty African sun."

It is tempting to say that "symbolically" France is seeking a sense of herself, a sense of place, of belonging, but I believe such an assumption is not sustained by either the character or the film as a whole. For throughout the film, France has an almost inscrutable facial expression. She does not express emotion. Rather, she watches and observes. France's significance as the obvious stand-in for director Denis may well have less to do with the obvious autobiographical connection between them than the position of observation that France embodies. France watches at a distance, always somewhat removed from what is going on about her. This is only partially the result of her status as a woman in Africa who is neither native nor tourist; it is also a function of the very nature of Denis's perspective as a filmmaker.

As played by the actress Mireille Perrier, France is conventionally pretty, but she does not do what conventionally pretty women usually do in the cinema: smile. Indeed, France's looks (in both senses of the term) are ambiguous, since she appears to be a typical leading lady, but she does not act as one expects leading ladies to act. She doesn't say please or thank you; she doesn't ingratiate herself to those around her. She doesn't apologize for being a white woman in Africa. Since France does not embody the characteristics typically associated with a conventionally attractive leading lady, it is tempting to place her in the dichotomous position of the femme fatale, the deceptive, dangerous woman whose failure to fit into a standard feminine role is a threat to the established order. There is nothing in the film to suggest France's status as the binary opposite of the typical leading lady, but the point is this: France is not a type of leading lady that we are used to seeing, not only because she does not fall into either extreme of the Madonna or the whore, but also because she is stripped of the kinds of typically feminine behavior that identify female characters to their audiences.

Only at one point in the film does France act as we might expect a leading lady to act. Near the conclusion of the film, France asks Mungo Park if he would like to have a drink, and she smiles very subtly, very slightly. France seems to flirt with the man, but the scene is also played as a low-key, ambiguous evocation of a desire for connection. The scene has its obvious corollary in the key scene in France's childhood when Protée encourages her to burn her hand, and the connection is reinforced by Park's examination of France's palm, where he—and we—see that the burn marks have remained like a tattoo, a permanent reminder of the connection between the white European and the black African. Mungo Park functions in this scenario as a man who evokes the past, because he is black, but who remains at a remove from it, because he is a stranger in Cameroon, because he is not African. Yet he says no to France, in an evocation of Protée who says no to Aimée. If Aimée and, to a lesser extent, France seek a sexual connection with a black man, the film does not in any way celebrate or romanticize that desire. In France's case, the brief emergence of a smile and an invitation to the man evokes a personal history of intimacy and loss in relationship to Protée.

As I've noted, *Chocolat* begins with a scene on the beach, during which the adult France observes a man and boy in the ocean. The film opens with a still image of the ocean as seen from the beach, and as the credits begin to roll, the image comes to life with movement and sound. What appeared to be a speck in the water is a young boy and an older man who emerge from the surf. The two frolic in the water and begin to exit frame left just as the camera begins to pan, left to right, moving from the water to the vantage point of a young woman, France, seated on the beach, casually watching the man and boy and listening to music via headphones. The movement of the father and son out of frame and the subsequent beginning of the tracking shot occur when Claire Denis's name appears on screen. The director's name is announced, in other words, at two crucial moments in the exposition of the film: the departure of the human subjects from the frame and the beginning of a shot that will reveal a female onlooker. In the subsequent shots, the young woman continues to observe the man and the boy, but what we see is no longer a long shot of two bodies but rather beautifully composed close-ups, first of the young boy's head as he lies in the sand, then of his hand as the surf and sand spill over it, and then of him and his father lying side by side (figs. 3, 4, 5, 6).

If the first image of the film captured the young woman's point of view, these images are pure cinema; they take the viewer away from the somewhat distant observer and into an intimate and glorious portrait of the body. These shots of black males, whom we might assume to be African, are certainly shaped by the onlooking view of the woman on the beach, yet they are more than that, for the close-ups of the boy's face and hand are, initially, out of sync with the images that precede them. Indeed, this is one of the central preoccupations of the film: a white woman can look and observe and attempt to make sense of her past, but there is always a beauty, a reality, and an experience that are beyond her grasp. The childhood house that France debates about seeing again is forever lost; the love she had for Protée is too defined within colonial life to ever exist autonomously.

Figure 3: The opening scene of *Chocolat* |

Figure 4: The opening scene of *Chocolat*

Figure 5: The opening scene of *Chocolat*

Figure 6: The opening scene of *Chocolat* |

The flashback section of the film ends when the plane is finally able to leave, taking the visitors away, and shortly after our return to the present tense of the film, France too makes her departure. After she leaves Mungo Park, France appears at the window of an airport. As she looks through the blinds, she smiles, and this time the smile is more emphatic than when she appeared to be flirting with the American man. The smile is enigmatic, and it initiates France's disappearance from the frame and from the film (fig. 7). We then cut to the reverse field of France's vision: a group of three men, all black Africans, load sculptures and other works of art onto a plane. As Abdullah Ibrahim's song "African Market" begins, we watch the men as they work and then take a break, all the while talking and joking among themselves. The camera approaches them in a tracking shot but stops short of framing them in close-up (fig. 8). They remain, rather, at a distance, their backs turned toward the camera (one of the men urinates, recalling a scene in the flashback section of the film when Protée and Marc urinate at the side of a road). The scene lasts just over three minutes, which is not necessarily such a long time, but one might well expect to see France's departure as the conclusion of the film. She, however, simply disappears after looking through the window, and what we see here exceeds what is introduced or framed by her vision. The final images and sounds of

Figure 7: France at the conclusion of *Chocolat* |

Figure 8: The conclusion of *Chocolat* |

the film, then, are not France, or even what France saw, but rather what France might have seen.

The conclusion could well be France's fantasy (one of the three transport workers is played by Isaach de Bankolé, the actor who plays Protée), and it could just as easily be the perspective of filmmaker Denis acquiring and then surpassing France's perspective. The interactions between the three men are "visible," certainly, but also distant, not quite within the grasp of the white French woman. The desire to see, coupled with the inevitable colonization of the look, provides the conclusion of the film, the creation of a liminal space in which colonialism has far from disappeared, but where the white female figure does not possess absolute power or knowledge. In this sense the film has come full circle, with the white woman's look suspended while black male bodies inhabit the screen. The look of the camera may well transcend that of France, whether offering a poetically abstract image of a child's body or a beautifully framed shot of three African men interacting with each other. Yet it is still France's position as observer that frames these images. France leaves Cameroon, and the men whose movements and interactions we observe seem free, in their camaraderie, but also still defined by the colonial relation, in that the work they do involves the export of "exotic" art objects.

In response to an interviewer's query ("It seems to me we see Protée is one of the workers at the airport"), Denis replied that initially, France was to have had the vague sensation that one of the transport workers looked like Protée. The idea was dropped because "I was afraid it would have too strong of a symbolic value. During filming, Isaach wanted to be one of the baggage handlers. I accepted his wish, I told him just to be a part of the group. I didn't do anything to make him recognizable, but I didn't do anything to hide his identity either. We'll see what happens" (Gili 1988: 16). For all that has been written about *Chocolat,* this particular detail has received little attention. Yet in Denis's conception of the film, this particular scene was a constant, no matter how many times she reworked the screenplay. "When you are a foreigner in a country, you travel, you see many new things, many exotic things. And for some reason, one little event will make you understand a lot. Very often as I was leaving, looking through the plane window, I would see guys working on the tarmac. I knew I was leaving, and I knew this was, like, his everyday life. And I thought, all of my romantic dreams of Africa always end with this kind of image, so real: people working, taking a pee, eating a sandwich, on a coffee break, rain starts falling. . . . As a foreigner, you have an image of what you want to see, and sometimes the reality is just, like . . . you just see something and you say, 'Ah, This is it. This is not my dream.' That was the airport scene for me" (Jones 1992: 15).

Denis's second narrative feature (after the documentary *Man No Run*, on the Cameroonian music group Les Têtes Brûlées) is *No Fear, No Die* (1990). In sharp contrast to *Chocolat, No Fear, No Die* has received far less critical attention than any other of Denis's films. Certainly the film is markedly different in tone than Denis's first feature, most strikingly because it looks so different: shot with a handheld camera, the film often straddles a potentially uncomfortable boundary between intimacy and claustrophobia. As a result, the characters of the film acquire nearly exaggerated personae.

Set in Rungis, an entry point into the city for food and produce in the somewhat desolate outskirts of Paris, *No Fear, No Die* is concerned with the parallel yet sharply divergent journeys of two men, Dah (Isaach de Bankolé) and Jocelyn (Alex Descas), who are seeking their fortunes through a business arrangement with Ardennes (Jean-Claude Brialy), a somewhat shady and unsavory French entrepreneur who wishes to exploit Jocelyn's experience in training roosters for cockfighting. Whereas *Chocolat* takes Denis's own experiences growing up in Cameroon as a point of departure, there is virtually nothing autobiographical about *No Fear, No Die.* Nonetheless, Denis's own relationship to this film embodies something of the detached observer that we see France become at the ending of *Chocolat,* and yet a sense of intimate relationship remains as well. For at the center of *No Fear, No Die* are relationships between men, particularly the friendship between Dah and Jocelyn, and the intimacy and identification between Jocelyn and the cocks he trains. Women are deliberately excluded from this world, but for that very reason they are never really absent.

No Fear, No Die is a film that emerged from a sad loss, the death from AIDS of a common friend of Denis and Descas and Bankolé (the actors are friends in real life). Denis began *No Fear, No Die* by writing the scene near the end of the film when Dah is cleaning the body of his dead friend. "I felt how difficult it is to say goodbye to people who are dying in a hospital. There is no more contact. I remember in my childhood, when people were dying, there was what we call 'la toilette du mort'—a way to say goodbye for the last time. . . . That was the first scene I imagined and the story grew around that, which was rather awkward" (Jones 1992: 11). Having begun the film in this way, Denis felt a certain finality, and there is indeed a sense of mourning throughout the film.

Denis might have had reservations about any attempt on the part of a white director to represent an African point of view in *Chocolat*, but *No Fear, No Die* has a first-person narrator, Dah, whose voice-over appears at the beginning of the film and frequently throughout. A first-person voice-over narration does not mean that the film "belongs" to Dah, but it does mean that he possesses knowledge and serves as the entry into the film for the spectator. But the narration seems to come from a different Dah, one who is observing himself and his friend, or perhaps it is an internal reflection, an effect heightened by the fact that, initially, we do not see Dah's face, but rather the back of his head. His first spoken words in the film are striking: "I am black and my friend is the same color. He's West Indian and I'm Beninese." At the beginning of the film, Dah meets his friend Jocelyn to pick up a shipment of roosters to be prepared for fighting. Dah is driving, and the scene takes place at night so that his face and Jocelyn's are difficult to see.

The close range of the camera accentuates the darkness of the image. Dah's statement of the obvious, that he is black and so is his friend, might appear to be curious words with which to begin the film. To whom is Dah speaking? If it seems obvious that he is providing the spectator with information—and quite a bit of exposition is given in the opening moments of the film, before the credits roll—there is nonetheless something in Dah's narration that goes beyond exposition. Dah's voice seems firm, clear, coherent, as if summarizing for a bystander—the film's spectator—the backstory of the film. Yet Dah's allusion to his friend, whom we do not see immediately, suggests that the first-person narration by Dah is always shared with his friend. For just before the credits roll, Dah's voice-over is suddenly situated very firmly within the connection between him and Jocelyn: "you're the expert," he says to Jocelyn, and the latter man smiles. Dah puts a tape into the truck's tape player and the credits begin against the background of Bob Marley's song "Buffalo Soldier."

The role of Dah is played by Isaach de Bankolé, familiar to viewers of *Chocolat* as the actor who played Protée. Dah's voice-over, with its attendant function of commenting upon and summarizing what the spectator sees, also suggests Dah's function in relationship both to Jocelyn and to Ardennes. Dah handles the money and the business transactions, while Jocelyn trains the roosters. Rarely does Jocelyn speak in the film; rather, he expresses himself in the choreography of the training of the birds. Dah watches out for Jocelyn throughout the film, and occasionally Dah cites words of wisdom from his friend.

Ardennes runs a restaurant and lodges Dah and Jocelyn in its basement, along with the roosters. Ardennes has converted part of an unused building into a cockfight arena. Ardennes has a connection with Jocelyn, whom he knew as a child in the Antilles when he had a relationship with Jocelyn's mother. At several points there are suggestions by Ardennes that he could have been Jocelyn's father, and at other key moments it is clear that Jocelyn's mother is a romanticized and idealized figure for Ardennes.

Ardennes's household consists of his young wife, Toni, and his adult son (by another wife), Michel, as well as various employees. There is an upstairs/downstairs quality in the arrangement of the space of the restaurant, with Ardennes and his family situated upstairs, where we see them in the restaurant, and Dah and Jocelyn downstairs. Toni is curious about the two men and the roosters, and we learn, both through Dah's narration and the actual events of the film, that she ventures downstairs at several points. Ardennes's interest in the cockfighting is clearly financial, whereas for Jocelyn the training of the cocks is an art form, and he is defined, throughout the film, in close proximity to the animals. This is both the beauty of his character and his undoing. For Jocelyn undergoes a descent, whereby the rituals of the training of the cocks become deadly. Jocelyn's special rooster provides the name of the film, yet he—the rooster—is sacrificed relatively early in the film, thus marking a strong sense both of Jocelyn's identification with the animal, and a premonition of what is to come for Jocelyn. (The English translation of *S'en Fout la mort*—*No Fear, No Die*—might be more appropriately translated as "to hell with death.")

Virtually every aspect of cockfighting in the film has an intensely symbolic dimension. Cockfighting means something quite different to

Jocelyn than it does to Ardennes, although both share the hope of making money. For Jocelyn, the preparation of the cocks for fighting and the fights themselves are part of a cultural tradition that is virtually alien to Ardennes, except as a tourist. Ardennes is a gambler, and the passion with which he speaks of betting on the birds is matched only by the passion he expresses for Jocelyn's mother. Ardennes seeks to make money both from Jocelyn's expertise and from a largely immigrant audience eager to enjoy a spectacle evocative of other times and other places.

Thus cockfighting stands for the colonial encounter itself; what was part of West Indian culture is uprooted and commodified so that the French businessman can make money. Cockfighting has obvious sexual dimensions. Toni's curiosity about the cocks is also a curiosity about Jocelyn, and the white men in the film act out of a sexual jealousy that can barely be sublimated in their management of the cockfighting; their control over the birds, the black men, and the white woman is ultimately limited.

As the sacrificial figure in this intersection of race and sexuality, Jocelyn embodies much of the film's complexity. As the trainer of the birds, he is masterful, but there is something soft and easy about his movements, as if he is being led by the birds as much as the birds are following his orders. In other words, if rational Dah holds their relationship together, Jocelyn is far more unstable, not only in the obvious terms of his eventual breakdown but also in terms of his intimate identification with the birds. Jocelyn is the threat posed to the white man, particularly as embodied in Michel, the white son who acts out a quintessentially (but oddly inverted) oedipal triangle when he stabs Jocelyn to death in the pit. Jocelyn becomes increasingly fragile in the film, and Dah reports that Jocelyn is obsessed with "having" Toni (he names a white bird "Toni" as some kind of compensation). Only near the end of the film does Jocelyn—drunk and flailing wildly in the pit—actually touch Toni; when he lunges for her, Michel stabs him. The fighting of the cocks thus suggests the acting out of the rage that is otherwise contained—at least for a time—in the film.

In creating a set of actions so shaped by both colonialism and sexuality, Claire Denis draws upon the ways in which Frantz Fanon has theorized the psychic toll of colonialism. While Fanon is never mentioned by name in the film, Denis has acknowledged in interviews that the film was directly inspired by her reading of Fanon. "It's a film that's influenced by Frantz Fanon's *Black Skins, White Masks,*" said Denis. "I understood something in Fanon's book that touched me immensely. . . . Fanon describes a special type of neurosis—colonized people feeling psychologically defeated even though they are physically free to determine their future" (Reid 1996: 69). The characterization of Jocelyn is most indebted to Fanon, and the dominant contours of Jocelyn's fall have to do with the destabilization of his position in terms of cockfighting, as well as in his relationship with Ardennes and Toni. In each case Jocelyn loses himself, particularly insofar as his own subjectivity is concerned, and he embodies the "alienated psyche" so central to Fanon's discussion of subject/object relationships in the interactions between whites and blacks. The cocks are not just beautiful animals that he trains, or even extensions of himself; rather, they *are* him. Toni is desirable but inaccessible, and the inaccessibility becomes all-encompassing for Jocelyn, just as Ardennes's racist idealization of Jocelyn's mother becomes internalized. Throughout the film Ardennes speaks of Jocelyn's mother in romanticized, idealized terms. As Denis herself has said, "It's really a cliché of post-colonialism—the only woman I loved was an exotic woman, there could never be a better love than an exotic love" (Jones 1992: 14).

Ardennes's idealization of the West Indian woman has effects on the members of his own family; his son Michel mentions that during his entire life, Jocelyn's mother was Ardennes's obsession. Ardennes's current family, seemingly so white and so French, is not the polar opposite of the woman Ardennes knew in Martinique but rather has been shaped by Ardennes's idealization of her. The revelation of the dependence between the white family and the black woman occurs in a key scene in the film. After a cockfight, a dinner is served. François, the black chef in the restaurant, prepares the dead cock's body to serve to the guests (Ardennes thinks this is West Indian custom, but he is wrong) (Bouzet 1990: 22). Unusually, Jocelyn and Dah have joined Ardennes, Toni, and Michel at the table (previously, Dah turned down an invitation to eat with the French family, saying that he and Jocelyn prefer to eat their own food, by themselves). As is the case throughout the film, the scene is shot in medium close-ups with a handheld camera, so that there is a simultaneous sense of closeness and unease. Ardennes sits next to his son, and across the table from Dah and Jocelyn. He speaks in elegiac terms of Jocelyn's mother. Jocelyn looks at Ardennes but does not speak, and Ardennes tells him that he has the same look, the same gaze, as his mother. Throughout the film, Dah and Jocelyn both are defined as observers looking on, and scenes are often drawn to introduce the viewer to what is seen through the perspective of one of the two (indeed, it is Jocelyn's view of Ardennes and Toni that provides the introduction to this scene). But here, and perhaps none too convincingly, Ardennes attempts to possess that gaze by sexualizing it, by claiming that he sees his idealized lover in Jocelyn's eyes.

Much has been made of the function of the look in Fanon's work, of how the colonial encounter is, precisely, a relationship of seeing and non-seeing, whereby the colonial subject relegates the colonized to a position of both pure object and non-object simultaneously. Fanon refers to the specific example of how, when white people adopt the equivalent of pidgin English to speak to blacks, no matter what their intentions, "it is just this absence of wish, this lack of interest, this indifference, this automatic manner of classifying him, imprisoning him, primitivizing him, decivilizing him, that makes him angry" (Fanon 1967: 32). Ardennes's insistence on mastery is specifically linked to his own sexual desire for Jocelyn's mother, and her son thus becomes fixed, by Ardennes, in the position of sexual object. Ardennes cannot look at Jocelyn without seeing Jocelyn's mother, and so Jocelyn's own perspective becomes alienating until, eventually and unsurprisingly, he becomes fixated upon Toni, Ardennes's wife.

Toni, however, does not completely conform to the stereotype of the white woman who desires the black man as an expression of her own racial privilege. Nor does Jocelyn's attraction to Toni unfold quite as one might expect. From her first appearance in the film, Toni is presented as Ardennes's possession, and the dynamics of sexual and racial possession are subtly juxtaposed. Toni's status as a desirable yet unattainable (for anyone but Ardennes) woman is enhanced by the fact that actress Solveig Dommartin's best-known role is the beautiful trapeze artist Marion in Wim Wenders's film *Wings of Desire* (1987) (for which Claire Denis was first assistant director). Toni is introduced after Ardennes has given Dah and Jocelyn a tour of the building where they will put the cocks on display when he leads them into the restaurant—called, as if for emphasis, "Chez Toni." As she works behind the bar, Ardennes grabs her and says to the men: "Isn't my Toni beautiful?" Close-ups and the moving camera reveal the exchange of looks between Ardennes, Dah, and Jocelyn. Ardennes is proclaiming: "this is my woman," but perhaps more interestingly, Jocelyn and Dah also possess active looks in the scene and observe Ardennes's display as much as the woman herself. Tellingly, immediately after the introduction of Toni, Ardennes leads the two men into the kitchen and presents François, his black chef, and jokes with him in a familiar, if condescending, way. Ardennes seems to declare: this is my woman, this is my chef; this is my building; you are now my employees and I am escorting you to the basement, through warrens and dark corridors, where you will be out of sight.

Toni's later appearances in the film occur almost exclusively when she is either confronting or seeking out Dah and/or Jocelyn. Shortly after the introduction of Toni, we see Dah walking toward the door of the restaurant from the outside, carrying a plastic tray for François and various items he has purchased for the cocks. Toni speaks to him through the glass and gestures at him to go around to the back (here she is an echo of Ardennes, who in one of his early interactions with Dah and Jocelyn tells them to use the back entrance). The restaurant is closed for a family dinner, but Toni's expression conjures up, even if very briefly, the racist response of a white woman seemingly afraid of the potential invasion of her space by a black man (fig. 9). The family dinner is shaped by class and race distinctions. Once Dah has come inside, Toni asks François, the chef, to make her a cup of coffee. If the brief expression on Toni's face initially suggests hostility, then a later scene makes the hostility obvious. Toni comes downstairs to complain about the loud music that Dah and Jocelyn use as accompaniment for the training of the cocks. In all of these scenes, from Toni's first appearance, to the threshold encounter with Dah at the door, to the confrontation in the basement, Toni is clearly separated from the two men—by the bar, by the glass of the door, by the space of the basement room itself.

Toni's position begins to shift when her presence is mediated through Dah and Jocelyn. Dah goes to the bar of the restaurant and describes in voice-over how he sometimes takes a break to see what is going on in the restaurant. He observes Toni working at the bar, having a somewhat flirtatious conversation with Michel. Then Dah says in his voice-over

Figure 9: Toni and Dah in *No Fear, No Die* |

narration: "Toni's a strange girl" ("Toni, c'est une fille bizarre"), and he describes how she—despite Ardennes's wishes—sometimes comes down to the basement to watch them. Dah then goes on to describe Jocelyn's philosophy that females in any form—women or hens—are bad for cockfighting. In the dinner scene discussed previously, Jocelyn's look at Toni and Ardennes provides the visual frame for the scene. Jocelyn's position as silent observer becomes more pronounced when we see Toni in the basement, attempting to touch one of the birds (the bird—like Jocelyn—is resistant to touch; all she manages to get is a feather). Michel has followed her there, and we see the most concrete evidence thus far in the film of their sexual relationship. Although Toni resists his advances, it is clear that the two of them have a sexual relationship. Jocelyn and Dah walk downstairs, and Jocelyn observes the two.

If Dah observes the world around him from a distance, Jocelyn cannot. The film's mise-en-scène does not make entirely explicit the attraction that Jocelyn feels toward Toni; rather, it is Dah's narration that makes the point, emphasizing his role as observer. Claire Denis is a mistress of understatement, and it is not surprising that in a film so preoccupied with the violence that lurks beneath the surface of human gestures and behaviors, the connection between Jocelyn and Toni is suggested rather than made explicit. Toni herself is an observer of Jocelyn and Dah, and Jocelyn in particular, but virtually always when Jocelyn is accompanied by one of the cocks, emphasizing once again how his identity is so totally merged with the birds. One of the most disturbing scenes in the film occurs when Jocelyn begins dancing with one of his birds to the accompaniment of the same music that caused Toni's outburst earlier. Dah observes the scene and tells Jocelyn that he is going too far, that his behavior is out of control. In the background of the image stands Toni, holding a fake leopard skin coat, with a cheesy painting of a black woman in the "tropics" creating a backdrop for her as Jocelyn leaves the room, and a backdrop for Jocelyn's own alienation as well.

After a brief scene where Jocelyn and Dah take a break at a bar, we see yet another scene of dance and frenzy, now in the disco run by Michel. Jocelyn is dancing with a white woman, and he appears to enter a trancelike state that is sexualized but oddly detached from the present tense of the scene. Indeed, the woman appears to be a stand-in for one of the cocks that Jocelyn trains, evoking the previous scene where Dah warns Jocelyn he is out of control. Jocelyn clutches the woman, until she, with a minimum of facial expressions, pushes him away and stares at him, as if to ask him what exactly he is doing. Jocelyn bows to her, almost in a chivalrous manner, and walks off the dance floor. We then see Toni dancing, apparently by herself. Whatever the connection between Toni and Jocelyn, it is fragmented and displaced, and if the dark-haired white woman was a substitute for Toni and/or the birds, the film leaves Toni to dance by herself, emphasizing her connection to yet distance from Jocelyn.

If Frantz Fanon is one important source for *No Fear, No Die,* a second is the author whose words appear at the beginning of the film. The opening title cites the autobiography of African American writer Chester Himes, who lived in France for many years, and whose literary reputation in France has always been considerably greater than in the United States (where he is best known as the author of the novels upon which the films *Cotton Comes to Harlem* [1970] and *A Rage in Harlem* [1991] were based). The citation comes from *The Quality of Hurt,* the first volume of Himes's autobiography: "human beings—all human beings, of whatever race or nationality or religious belief or ideology—will do anything and everything" (1972: 3). Himes is referring specifically to his experiences in prison in the United States, and to the one lasting impression prison life made on him. He goes on to say that prison life convinced him that "I can never again be hurt as much as I have already been hurt" (1972: 3). At the beginning of his autobiography, Himes discusses not only prison life but also his decision to move to Europe. Although Himes is evoked only briefly in the film, the citation is important, for it suggests a common bond of race and exile between the writer and the two characters. Additionally, in his opening narration, Dah repeats the Himes quotation, with the preface that while he has been waiting in the car, a sentence repeats itself over and over in his mind. After reciting the words that we have just seen on screen, Dah says: "I forget who said it, but it's not important." Dah "forgets" who wrote the words, and if the authorship of the words isn't important, it is largely because Himes's statement applies to virtually everyone in the film.

Central to the relationship between Dah and Jocelyn is not only their shared experience of the Fanonian sense of the price of colonialism on psychic life, or Chester Himes's invocation—from prison—that people are capable of anything and everything, but also the fact that the knowledge suggested by both of these perspectives can be articulated only by Dah in the film. As a narrator, as the more rational of the two, as the "financial" side of the partnership, Dah knows what others do not. With Jocelyn, there is, in contrast, the troubled sense from the outset of the film that he is the friend who will not survive because he is "psychologically defeated" and has neither the distance nor the desire to step outside of the forces of commerce and colonialism.

Denis has described her admiration for John Cassavetes's film *Killing of a Chinese Bookie* (1976), in which Ben Gazzara plays the owner of a nightclub who owes gambling debts and who is forced to kill a Chinese criminal in order, presumably, to pay off his debts (although those who order him to perform the killing have no intention of letting him live). Shot at mostly close range with a handheld camera (as in *No Fear, No Die*), Cassavetes's film explores both the inevitability of death and the ways in which a person just keeps going in the face of such inevitability. Gazzara is wounded when he reaches his target (facing many more armed men than his creditors led him to believe), but he refuses to go to the hospital. Instead, he insists on returning to his club, where he enjoys an intimate relationship with his strippers and his other employees.

Running a club is what he does, and he insists upon being there even as his own decline is apparent. "When we were filming the death of Alex Descas [Jocelyn], . . . I was all the time thinking of that same death, this death which in the same way is expected, which brings relief but is also painful. I can say that *No Fear, No Die* could be dedicated to that film" (Ancian 2002: 3).

Death may well be inevitable for Jocelyn. He is killed as an intruder because he has encroached upon the presumed sanctity of white identity (that he is killed by the son who is having an affair with his father's wife is no small irony; racial boundary-crossing is apparently more threatening than quasi-incestuous relationships). Symbolically, the sacrifice of Jocelyn suggests the annihilation of any notion of art or beauty in the cockfight; it has become, purely and simply, a matter of commerce. Yet Jocelyn's interactions with the cocks provide some of the most beautiful scenes in *No Fear, No Die,* filmed at close range and following the movements of the man and the animal with focused intensity. Jocelyn's body moves in a kind of rhythmic dance of both oneness with and separation from the cocks. There are moments, when the cock flaps its wings, that some images from the "pre-cinematic" days of motion pictures come to mind, images like those of Etienne-Jules Marey's birds, as the capture of movement seems both intensely fast and curiously still, their wings fluttering yet immobile (fig. 10).

In both *Chocolat* and *No Fear, No Die,* an obvious symbolism reigns— "France" is the protagonist who seeks a relationship to her past, and Protée is, like the god he is named for, able to move quickly from one identity to another; the cockfight is sexual and racial in overdetermined ways (Affergan 1986, rpt. 1994; Geertz 1972; Dundes 1994). Yet while the symbolism could be regarded as verging on the heavy-handed, it never really is, largely because of the ways in which bodies and viewpoints are constantly on the move. There is never a secure, fixed position for the symbolic levels to sink in and determine how the various threads and components of the films function in relationship to each other. In both films bodies and places are solid and transitory at the same time.

In describing her work with the actors in *No Fear, No Die,* Denis has spoken specifically of how the sustained use of the handheld camera puts you "always in the present. It's very energetic. It's like a dance every day with the actors" (Jones 1992: 12). Denis has also said

Figure 10: Jocelyn and the choreography of the
birds in *No Fear, No Die*

that she doesn't have a "concept" for directing actors. "I see it more
like choreography. . . . Directing and acting exist in an organic relation
similar to a dance between director and actors" (Reid 1996: 72). At the
conclusion of *Chocolat*, the female protagonist literally leaves the scene,
and the perspective that develops at the end of the film is complex,
suggesting both a desire to see and a desire to remain at a distance. In
No Fear, No Die, however, watching and listening in create intimacy
for the spectator. The very nature of point of view has expanded in this
film from what we see in *Chocolat*, as if the conclusion of the earlier
film provided a point of departure for *No Fear, No Die*. If the director's
position vis-à-vis what she films is a fluid relationship, a choreography,
as Denis describes it, then the spectator too is engaged in that dance
between director and actors.

Strange Alchemies: *U.S. Go Home* and *Nénette and Boni*

The year 1994 was a busy one for Claire Denis. *I Can't Sleep* was presented at Cannes in May, and in July Denis began shooting *U.S. Go
Home*. The telefilm is one of nine episodes in the television series pro-

duced by ARTE, entitled *Tous les Garçons et les filles de leur âge* (All the Boys and Girls of Their Age). Based on an idea by Chantal Poupaud, the series was designed to elicit a sense of how, during different periods of French history, from the early 1960s to the late 1980s, French teenagers lived their lives, their dreams, their culture, and their history. Each episode in the series was required to include music from the era, and it had to include at least one party scene. In retrospect, one can hardly imagine requirements better suited to Claire Denis's cinematic imagination, in which music and dance play a dominant role. And indeed, Denis's sixty-four-minute film, *U.S. Go Home,* evokes how centrally music—and especially music from Britain and the United States—shaped French adolescence in the 1960s, and how dance is a ritual that allows a convergence, even if fleeting and temporary, of private and public selves. Initially, Denis was somewhat ambivalent about the project. "I could have said yes or no. I hated parties, but I was excited about the importance of music in the series. When I was an adolescent, my records and record player were my secret. Alone in my room, I listened to the Animals, the Yardbirds, Ronnie Bird. The idea of using their music was a powerful motivation to make the film" (Maveyraud 1994: 90). Denis's film is the second, timewise, in the series, situated in the mid-1960s (André Téchiné's *Le Chêne et le roseau* was the first episode, set in the early 1960s).[3] Denis wrote the screenplay for the film with Anne Wiazemsky, an actress well known for her appearances in Robert Bresson's *Au Hasard, Balthazar* (1966) and numerous films by Jean-Luc Godard, and who is also a successful novelist.

U.S. Go Home takes place in the outskirts of Paris, in a housing development near a U.S. military base. The images of the housing development and the surrounding areas give a sense of a kind of no-man's-land, where construction projects of one kind or another always seem to be under way, and where daily life is a constant ritual of self-invention in the midst of housing complexes with euphemistic names like "Iris Sauvages" (Wild Irises). (The name of the housing complex is a nod to Téchiné's film, but with the obvious difference that "roseaux sauvages" has a literary reference to Jean de la Fontaine's seventeenth-century fable *Le Chêne et le roseau [The Oak and the Reed]*; "wild irises" does not.) Martine (Alice Houri) and Alain (Grégoire Colin) live in an apartment with their mother. The premise of the film is simple: Martine wants to go to a party, and she begs her brother to accompany her and her best friend, Marlène (Martine's mother will not let her go unless her brother takes her). Martine has a single goal in mind: to lose her virginity.

In an area so near yet so far from an urban center, means of transport occupy a central part of the film, from the hitchhiking Marlène and Martine do to get from one place to another, to the bus they take with Alain to go to the party, to the car that leads, at the end of the film, to the fulfillment of Martine's desire. As in Denis's other films, movement and passage are key. The two friends leave Alain in the bus, for he has his own party to attend—one where, as Martine teases him earlier in the film, "on se couche" (people sleep around). When the two girls go to their party, a wonderful scene evokes their simultaneous apprehension, desire, and discomfort. They arrive at the house where the party is taking place but peek through the bushes that surround the house, like voyeurs not quite certain of what they want or what they are witnessing. Their faces show a sense of wonder, yet their voices express concern that the parents are present (and dancing with the teenagers, something they consider truly disconcerting). They decide to leave, and we next see them at the door to a house that is unlike anything we have yet seen—a large, imposing house, signifying the kind of wealth and privilege that are otherwise absent in the film. Martine tells the young man at the door (who is obviously much older than the two girls) that they are with Alain. This is one of many signs that Martine is at a kind of transitional point between a dependence on her brother and a desire for autonomy and independence.

At this party, although Martine and Marlène have gone inside, they still appear like outsiders. They are now wandering around in a world that obviously fascinates them, but within which they seem like somewhat stunned observers. When they find Alain, another dimension of the relationship between the three main characters emerges. Martine is excited to find her brother, almost like a child greeting a beloved parent, while Marlène's face suggests, for the first time, that her own relationship to her best friend's brother is defined by desire and jealousy. Indeed, Marlène looks sad and wistful as she watches Alain dance with another girl, and she quickly initiates an encounter with a boy by asking for a cigarette. He asks her to dance, and an extended scene on the dance floor reveals that Marlène is dancing for Alain, and that Alain himself may well have feelings for Marlène, as the two exchange glances across the bodies of their respective dance partners.

Martine, meanwhile, has little success in her own pursuit of sexual initiation. When she follows Marlène's lead by asking a boy for a cigarette, he tells her that her girlfriend is attractive and promptly says goodbye. An ongoing motif in Martine's quest and frustration is her continuous query to everyone she meets about where she can put her things. She doesn't quite know what to do with herself (or her things). Eventually, a boy asks Martine to dance, but when another boy (the same one who earlier told her Marlène was pretty) interrupts and proceeds to come on to her rather aggressively, Martine resists his advances. Clearly Martine's desire to lose her virginity is not as simple as she presented it initially to Marlène; she wants something else at the same time.

That "something else" is very much tied up with Martine's relationship with her brother, and the first element of the "something else" Martine discovers is, at first, profoundly disconcerting. As Martine begins wandering through the party, now looking for Marlène, she finds her friend, in a room, naked, with her brother. Psychoanalytic scenarios are not really central to Claire Denis's films, but this constitutes nonetheless something of a primal scene, for Martine seems like a hurt and wounded child as she witnesses what appears to be a failed sexual encounter between her brother and her best friend.

If dancing, throughout the film, seems to be defined primarily as a ritual of heterosexual desire, it takes on a somewhat different quality when Alain finds his sister after her discovery and comforts her by dancing with her. He is tender and consoling as he holds her in his arms. However, to appreciate fully the significance of this brother/sister encounter, we first need to consider what is undoubtedly one of the greatest dance scenes ever filmed. The first image of *U.S. Go Home* shows us Alain, sitting on his bed and reading aloud from a well-known text by Seneca, "On the Shortness of Life," about how giving in to one's sexual desires is a sign of weakness:

> Among the worst offenders I count those who give all their time to drink and lust; that is the sorriest abuse of time of all. Though the phantom of glory which possesses some men is illusory, their error, at all events, has a creditable look. And even if you cite the avaricious, the wrathful,

and those who prosecute unjust hatreds and even unjust war, these too are more manly kinds of sin. But the stain upon men abandoned to their belly and their lusts is vile. (Hadas 1965: 54)

Behind him is hideous, typically 1960s wallpaper with a geometric design, strategically decorated with record album covers. There is a certain nostalgia evoked in the décor as well as in the text that Alain reads aloud. It is as if, within the iconography of the 1960s, teenagers like Alain were finding their way amid both the music of the era and the philosophy they try on for size. In both cases, models of masculinity promise strength and power. If Seneca's philosophy gives Alain a model of masculine purity to emulate, dance gives him something else as well, a physical acting out of desire, frustration, and creativity.

Following this introduction to Alain, we see the landscape of the Wild Irises and the surrounding territory, accompanied by Martine's commentary in voice-over. She describes where she lives, and how Paris, barely visible through the fog, is located nearby but is too far to visit easily. Martine notes that the American military base is nearby, and that she and her friend Marlène hitchhike often. Her narration concludes: "I feel sheltered. My mother protects me, my brother protects me, even Marlène protects me." Our next view of Alain is in his bedroom, where he listens to "Hey Gyp" (by Eric Burdon and the Animals) and dances frenetically and wildly, as if he is possessed simultaneously by an identification with the music, sexual desire, and an uninhibited feeling of pure exuberance. Grégoire Colin is fabulous as he lets himself go in a complete and total identification with the music and the lyrics; he sings along with "I'm gonna buy you a Chevrolet" and poses with his cigarette, wildly flailing his arms and later imitating the shooting of a gun.

Compared with the opening image of Alain, the implication is obvious: dance allows him to be physical and sexual without the risks implied by the "weakness" of giving in to one's sexual desires, that is, without the interference of another person. The dance is a kind of state of suspended sexual animation, creating a sense of physical self and performance, while remaining independent of actual contact with another. Interestingly, once Alain stops dancing, he and we discover that Martine has been observing his dance, unbeknownst to him (and us). In a subtle way, the movement from Alain center stage, to the discovery of his sister watching him, suggests how interconnected the two are, not just in terms of their affection for each other, but also in terms of their own sexual identities. And here, we see Martine as an observer of her brother's ritualized dance, just as later in the film she will be an observer of the various dances at the two parties she attends.

Between the clutching of the bodies dancing at the party, and the solo performance of Alain at the beginning of the film, the dance between brother and sister constitutes a kind of bridge, a sense of real physical connection, a communication that is sensual and more intimate than a social ritual. Indeed, the dance between brother and sister is filmed differently from the dancing we see at the party. Unlike the tangled bodies and shadows of the dancing teenagers we see in close-ups dancing at the party, the bodies of the brother and sister are shown with both intimacy and detachment. We can see them clearly, and we can see the gestures of tenderness between them. The lighting is much more even than in other dance scenes in the film, where the emphasis tends to be on shadows, the interchangeability of bodies (marked in a curious way by the glances exchanged between Marlène and Alain as they dance with other people), and a constantly moving camera. The camera here is still and allows only a contemplation of a special and unique relationship. And in the overall structure of the film, this dance is indeed decisive, for it marks both the close connection between the two, and their separation. If dancing is a sexual connection, Martine is desperate to dance, and her brother is desperate *not* to (and certainly he seems resistant to Marlène's attraction to him). In this scene, then, the siblings connect through a dance that momentarily takes both of them out of their separate spheres.

In the final section of the film, Martine and Alain go their separate ways. Until this point, most of the film has been accompanied by numerous songs of the period. The songs acquire different functions in relationship to what we see on screen. Individual characters, for instance, are defined by their relationship to music—Alain, with "Hey Gyp," and Marlène and Martine with Ronnie Bird's elegy to Buddy Holly (in English) as they prepare for the party. Even Alain and Martine's mother—otherwise a minor character—has her own musical interlude. Early in the film, we see her humming along to "I Believe to My Soul" (by the Animals), and then she asks herself out loud: "What am I going to make for dinner?"

At other moments, the songs reiterate what we see on the image track. "Good Morning Little Schoolgirl" by the Yardbirds accompanies an image of Martine and Marlène and their friends as they wait for the school bus. Sometimes the songs provide an ironic commentary. When Marlène and Martine hitchhike, they are picked up by a man who first of all scolds them for hitchhiking and later tries to get them to have a drink with him; the song we hear is "Leader of the Pack"—"Le Chef de la Bande" sung in French by Frank Alamo. During the party, the juxtaposition of the songs with the images of the dancers creates a sense of both connection and distance from the music. For example, "Try a Little Tenderness" (by Otis Redding) is a classic "slow dance song," but its placement in the film occurs when Marlène and Alain are dancing with different partners, and the last thing that seems to characterize their relationship is "tenderness." And when Martine finds her brother and Marlène together, the accompanying song is "Bring It to Me," with the lyric "Bring your sweet loving home to me" (by the Animals). Given how preoccupied the film is with Martine's relationship to her brother, the song is a touching commentary both on what they share and what is about to separate them.

More obviously, of course, the two parties that Marlène and Martine attend are defined by the music that is played. The party scenes are shaped and structured by the movement from one song to the next and not just in the obvious sense that we are witnessing a party where one expects one song to follow another, one dance to follow another. Our introduction to the primary characters in the film occurs through particular pieces of music, and the development and flow of the interactions between these characters and the virtually faceless individuals we see in mobile close-ups occur through the juxtaposition of different songs.

All of these musical accompaniments are American or British, which, of course, corresponds to the music that was popular in Europe at the time. The first words of the film are from a broadcast of Radio Caroline, which Alain listens to before he begins his recitation of the Seneca text. Radio Caroline is a British offshore radio station that has been broadcasting popular music since the 1960s, and it is the station that Denis herself listened to as a teenager. The film does more with the Anglo-Saxon context than cite it as an example of "context." For beneath the French fascination with British and American music was profound ambivalence about the United States, in particular. When Denis was a teenager, she lived in an area not unlike that where Alain and Martine live, near an American military base. "I baby-sat for American families. I went to the base to buy records, jeans, and 'Fruit of the Loom.' But it was a contradictory dream because of the war in Vietnam. At the same time, we dreamed about American culture, literature, music, cinema, the American way of life. It was *the* influential country, but at the same time we were completely anti-American. We didn't hate Americans, but we were against the war in Vietnam, and we campaigned for peace" (Benjamin 1995: 10).

This ambivalence becomes one of the most important elements in the last section of the film. When Martine and Alain leave the party, there is a striking change in image and sound. Suddenly there is silence—that is, no music—and sounds of footsteps, conversation, cars, and the occasional rustlings of nature. Martine yells at her brother about how he treated Marlène; Alain tells her he wants them to walk home rather than hitchhike. They begin to walk and come upon an American soldier (Vincent Gallo), sitting in his car. This isn't the first time we have seen the soldier; at the beginning of the film, there is a brief image of him sitting next to his car, looking dejected. At the time, his image seems to suggest briefly the presence of the American military base mentioned in Martine's narration. When Martine and Alain happen upon the soldier after the party, Martine asks him for a ride, while Alain is less than enthusiastic (he says he doesn't want to have anything to do with an assassin). The soldier is a stereotypical American, in that he immediately calls Alain "Al" and insists that the two drink some of the Coca-Cola he has (on ice, no less) in the trunk of his car. Alain refuses, saying he is a communist and doesn't drink Coca-Cola.

Eventually Alain insists on being dropped off, and in close-up we see him walking home. In an extended sequence in the car, Gallo's soldier, Captain Brown, first acquires the solicitous, protective role associated with Alain toward Martine. Previously he was shocked when Martine asked for a beer (rather than a Coke), and he won't give her a cigarette (and asks if her mother knows she smokes). Martine engages in her own anti-Americanism, by chanting "U.S.A. Must Go Home" (the first specific allusion in the film to its title). But her chant seems less a taunt than a flirtation, and soon the attraction between the two becomes apparent. Observing how the camera moves in to focus on Gallo's cheek, which is throbbing ever so slightly, one critic notes how "only a great filmmaker attuned to bodies and their desires could have filmed so powerfully the American soldier's growing desire" (Bouquet 1994: 28).

In sharp contrast to the rest of the film, we hear only one song during the encounter between the American soldier and the French teenager, "Al Capone" by Prince Buster. As I've noted, other songs in the film provide commentary, sometimes ironic, on the encounters we see. In this instance, there appears to be a sharp contrast between the developing tenderness between Martine and Brown and the heavy beat and raucous lyrics of the song (punctuated by Prince Buster shouting "Don't call me Scarface, my name is Capone"). The driving beat and the shouted lyrics evoke "Hey Gyp," the song that accompanied Alain's stunning solo dance. There are other parallels between Alain and Brown, including a physical resemblance, but whereas Alain's body is expansive (especially when he is alone), there is a kind of reticence in Brown's movement. Yet Vincent Gallo has an imposing physical presence, so that one has the sense that there is something else going on beneath the surface. At the beginning of the film, Brown looks dejected, sitting next to his car, and when he resurfaces, he does not appear to have moved. Brown has his own dramas—could he be deserting the army?—but they are only suggested, never spelled out.

A beautiful accompaniment to the extended sequence in the car is the traveling shot of trees that are visible above and beyond the car. For once, the area where the film takes place seems beautiful, as if the surroundings are transformed by the interaction taking place between the two. Their sexual encounter, as well as the fulfillment of Martine's wish, takes place in a very subtle way. They stand in the dark and begin to embrace and then move out of the frame, so that the encounter occurs, literally, off-screen. Afterward, there is intimacy: Vido Brown (or Captain Brown, as he says his friends call him) drives the car and strokes Martine's face.

The contrast between the two scenes of sexual encounter is distinct.

At the party we see Marlène and Alain together, naked, in what could appear to be a stereotypical image of a sexual encounter (although the camera work here is very striking—the bodies are seen in close-up, but a close-up that moves, so that it is difficult to pin down the image, and given the darkness, difficult to read precisely what happens). But when Martine succeeds in losing her virginity, the event takes place entirely off-screen. Somewhat ironically, perhaps, the most tender moment of sexual encounter in the film is when Captain Brown caresses Martine's face.

The conclusion of the film is elliptical. It is dawn, and Marlène and Alain are waiting at the housing development. Are they waiting for Martine to return? Or simply waiting, in a kind of suspended state? Captain Brown's car arrives, Martine gets out, and he leaves. As he drives away, a wall with the words "US GO HOME" painted, graffiti-like, is revealed. We watch the three, Alain, Martine, and Marlène, standing there, and the only sound accompanying the shot is the chirping of birds. Indeed, in a film so saturated with music, this substitution of a different kind of "song" makes for a striking, poignant conclusion. We see close-ups of Martine and Marlène, and then a cut to the credits. We hear yet another song over the credits, "These Days," sung by Nico. This is the only time in the film that we hear a female vocalist. Given how little music is heard in the last section of the film, and how different this song is from the music in the rest of the film, Nico's voice announces a change in register and mood. This is not music meant for dancing, but rather for contemplation. Virtually all of the music in the film, with the brief exception of Ronnie Bird's tribute to Buddy Holly, has a dynamic quality of being in the present tense. Nico's song, because of her distinctively depressive voice (with her German accent), and because of the lyrics, is elegiac and mournful. The three teenagers are already achingly remembering what has just happened. Both girls have crossed a line, but the film chooses to frame them, finally, in a pose of contemplation, of suspension. And interestingly, while Alain is present in the medium shot of the three of them, there is no close-up of him at the end of the film, as if he has been, literally, displaced. But it is Marlène's face that we see in the last shot, the girl who also has been displaced by the triangle between Martine, Alain, and Captain Brown. Relationships shift, including that between brother and sister, and there is always someone, something—Marlène,

Captain Brown, music—to complicate their interactions. But in the end, the brother still waits for the sister, while the friend looks on.

Nénette and Boni is an entirely different film from *U.S. Go Home* in terms of characters and setting, but in many ways the film functions as a sequel to the earlier film. Produced by Dacia, a company that specializes in low-budget films with independent visions, it too is about the relationship between a brother and a sister. The film takes place in Marseille, where nineteen-year-old Boni (Grégoire Colin)—short for Boniface—lives in the house left to him by his mother; we don't know how or when she died. Boni makes pizzas for a living in a van given to him by an uncle, and in addition he traffics in stolen goods with a group of (male) friends who occasionally stay over at his apartment. Nénette (Alice Houri)—short for Antoinette—is fifteen years old. She lived with her father, from whom Boni is estranged, until her father placed her in a boarding school. Nénette has run away from school and gone to Boni's home. Nénette is pregnant, but we learn virtually nothing about how she became pregnant or who the father is. We have the sense (although this is never spelled out) that Nénette and Boni have not lived together for a very long time.

The relationship of *Nénette and Boni* to *U.S. Go Home* stemmed from Denis's desire to work again with Colin and Houri. "I felt like I just barely discovered them in *U.S. Go Home*," Denis said. "I was working on another film, based on a book, but I really wanted to work with them again." The opportunity allowed Denis to continue her exploration of brother-sister relationships. "Personally, I am the oldest child in the family," noted Denis, "and my younger brother will always be my little brother, even though now he is a grown man with children! And when he talks to me, I'm still his big sister" (Guilloux 1997: 28). Denis worked with her usual collaborators, Jean-Pôl Fargeau and Agnès Godard. The film is set in Marseille, where Fargeau lives (in the same neighborhood as Boni). Although Denis has continuously worked with some of the same actors in her films, *Nénette and Boni* is nonetheless unusual in that Colin and Houri are playing what might be called adaptations of the characters they played in *U.S. Go Home*.

An observer of the production of the film noted that Denis tended to direct her actors in terms of their bodies, not in terms of their lines. Grégoire Colin, describing Denis as a director for whom actors are not "clay to be molded," explained her direction as follows: "Claire just says one or two things, little things to help me understand Boni at that particular moment, and then it's up to me to do what I want, as I feel it should be done, even though we are doing far less improvising than on *U.S. Go Home,* where the scenario was only a few pages long" (Bouquet 1996: 58). Denis too described *Nénette and Boni* as a film with more constraints than her previous films. "The blending of dream and reality, without knowing which is which (something I'm committed to), reinforced the heaviness of the film" (Bouquet 1996: 55).

While *Nénette and Boni* is obviously the product of Denis's fascination with the brother-sister bond, another factor was influential in the creation of the film. In *U.S. Go Home,* the sister has her first sexual experience; in *Nénette and Boni,* the girl is pregnant. Denis was inspired to write *Nénette and Boni* not only to extend the brother and sister story of *U.S. Go Home* but also to explore the phenomenon of "accouchement sous X," which means, literally, anonymous birth, but the "sous X"—under X—also suggests a mark of erasure (Adler 1997). This form of birth requires a contract; all of the mother's expenses are paid, provided that she establish a kind of counterfeit identity for herself, one of anonymity. The process requires that the mother agree never to attempt to see the child, and the law is one of the more archaic in France—it was used during the Vichy regime, for instance, to assure a high birth rate.

Nénette and Boni begins with a brief scene of a white man selling counterfeit telephone cards to a group of black immigrants. There is a tight shot of the man selling the cards, and then the camera moves around the room, pausing on an individual before continuing. The movement of the camera is deliberate; we are close to the individuals, but we really cannot tell where they are (there is no establishing shot). Claire Denis has described the function of this scene as akin to looking through a pair of binoculars: "we begin looking around before we focus on what we want to see" (Strand 1997: 4). Although the main point of the film is, of course, the brother and sister, the counterfeit phone card reference returns three times in the film. The counterfeiter takes a picture of a man's phone card at the train station (when Nénette arrives in Marseille to find her brother). While he tells the man that his daughter collects phone cards and that he has never seen one like his, the counterfeiter obviously is taking the photograph in order to retrieve the number.

There is an echo, even if slight, with Nénette and her own father, for her father's connection with his children is, if not counterfeit, at the very least not what his children want or need.

Later, we see a Vietnamese woman using a pay phone, and later still, a connection is made between her and an administrator whom Nénette sees about giving up her baby for adoption. This woman's telephone bill has suddenly been overrun by calls to Ho Chi Minh City, and her interview with Nénette is interrupted when she speaks to a telephone company representative to complain. The intrusion, as it were, of the phone calls to Vietnam with counterfeit cards, and of the phone call from the telephone company, serves to underscore Nénette's own precarious position. It is too late in her pregnancy for her to have an abortion, so her most logical choice is the "accouchement sous X," or anonymous birth.

These apparently random connections with a counterfeit telephone card scheme in *Nénette and Boni* suggest the importance of the unexpected connection in Denis's work. Individual characters are not defined "in depth," in any kind of psychological sense, but rather as always constructed in the process of becoming as they move through different spaces and places. Just as the relationship between the random and the determined is always in flux, so, too, is the boundary between center and margin, whether the center is defined in social, narrative, or cinematic terms.

Like *U.S. Go Home,* the overall style of *Nénette and Boni* is both intimate and detached. The camera moves to such an extent that stillness itself becomes something to remark upon. The camera and accompanying effects of editing create flow in *Nénette and Boni:* flow in the sense of camera movement, of a mobile vision; flow in the sense of never staying pinned down to a single subject for too long; and flow in the sense of creating a strong sense of connection between different spaces. Flow is established literally in the opening scenes of the film. In the first scene, the camera moves quickly across a group of people as the man tells his suspicious audience, when they ask why he should be trusted, that the cards are real: "They're real cards—look!" Of course, the cards are real in a material sense, but they also are fake, and the film is located precisely in that gap between what is apparent, material, and real, and what is real in the sense of valid and legitimate. Nénette's "illegitimate" child provides the occasion for a complete redefinition of what counts as a legitimate relationship, particularly in terms of family bonds.

After this short scene of the man selling counterfeit telephone cards, the titles of the film appear. The words "Nénette et Boni" are white against a black background, and they then dissolve, the letters now like ripples of water, into a solid black background. Then the image of Nénette appears, shot from above, as she is floating, Ophelia-like, her hair spread out and her eyes closed, in a swimming pool, shot from above. The music of the Tindersticks accompanies our view of Nénette as she opens her eyes and moves in the water. This is one of the only moments in the film where the fifteen-year-old seems happy, even if only momentarily. From Nénette standing next to the pool, there is a cut to close-ups of a young man driving a car. Here, the movement is fast and choppy, and we hear the loud noise of the racing car. The music of the Tindersticks continues, almost incongruously, as the driver and his passenger—Boni—enjoy careening around the city and calling out to the neighborhood *boulangère* (proprietress of the local bakery). The persistence of the music makes a link between sister and brother, but it also suggests, in this, our first view of Boni, that raucousness and rambunctiousness are not all that there is to his character.

From this initial encounter with Boni, we move to his home where he reads aloud from his diary (the scene is very evocative of Alain's reading aloud of Seneca in *U.S. Go Home*). Our initial impression of Boni is that he is completely driven by his sexual fantasies about the woman who runs the neighborhood bakery with her husband. We hear in detail about what he wants to do to her, and how he imagines sexual encounters with her, virtually always in torrid and somewhat violent terms. Yet the way in which his fantasies are presented is a bit more complex than simple masturbatory scenarios. Boni's diary is kept in a typical French student's notebook, and Boni's handwriting looks youthful, even childish. In the first passage that Boni reads aloud from the notebook, the sexual conquest of the woman gives way very quickly to an angry rant against his father, who left him and his mother. "Confessions of a loser," the entry is titled. "I, Boni Pavone, Pizzamaker, living in the house of my poor mother in the Canet, the fourteenth arrondissement of Marseille, wallowing in pornographic fantasies about a woman with a husband and three children . . ." Boni continues to describe what he would like to do to the woman, but the diary is as much about his family as about his sexuality. He swears on the grave of his mother that nothing will stop him from fulfilling his fantasies. He says that if he doesn't complete his mission—the sexual conquest of the woman—he will be branded a coward, just like the father who abandoned him and his mother.

The object of Boni's desires is played by Valéria Bruni-Tedeschi, and she is referred to as "la boulangère" throughout the film, echoing Marcel Pagnol's classic 1938 film *La Femme du boulanger,* in which Ginette Leclerc plays the sexy wife of the local baker (Strand 2001). The setting in Marseille makes the imprint of Pagnol even more emphatic, and Denis said in an interview that Pagnol was a "godfather" for the film (*Interview with Claire Denis*). There also are allusions to Jean Cocteau's *Les Parents terribles,* in terms of the relationship between brother and sister (and at one point, in a direct quotation, Nénette feeds her brother mashed bananas [Hurst 1997: 27]). One scene in the film alludes to Jacques Demy's 1961 film *Lola,* when an American soldier meets a waitress. These allusions attest, perhaps, to the strong awareness in Denis's films of French film history, but they also suggest what one critic calls a "generosity of admiration" (Lefort 1997).

One of Boni's vivid fantasies about the woman gives way to a scene of Boni in bed, smiling contentedly, and one assumes that the look of pleasure is due to the successful completion of his fantasy. We hear water running, and its source becomes clear only once the camera shows us the object of Boni's contented demeanor: his new coffee pot, with a built-in clock and timer. The use of sound is masterful in this scene. The guttural sounds of imaginary sexual satisfaction blend into those of a coffeepot gurgling. In the first instance, Boni's fantasies merge into mourning for his mother and rage at his father; in the second, there is a smooth movement from sexual gratification to domestic bliss. Indeed, Boni strokes the coffeepot as if it were a very agreeable lover. It would be a mistake to downplay Boni's active and rich sexual fantasy life, but the film gives us numerous indications that it isn't necessarily, or primarily, sexual satisfaction that Boni is after; there is "something else" there. In both of the examples cited here, the "something else" has to do with the comforts of home—his mother, and an appliance. If *Nénette and Boni* is a sequel to *U.S. Go Home,* it is also something of an inversion of the plot, for here the brother's desire for that "something

Seeing Others | 73

else" is central, whereas in the earlier film, it was the sister's desire that drove the film.

Although Nénette and Boni do not actually meet until thirty minutes into the film, the editing establishes connections between them as we move back and forth between Boni's work and his sexual fantasies, and Nénette's departure from school and arrival in Marseille. The film makes connections between them even when the two of them are separate—from Boni's happy interlude with the coffeemaker, for instance, we cut to Nénette preparing to leave school, and an imaginary shot counter-shot is established between them. Nénette shows up at Boni's home, but he does not appear to see her when he leaves to get the pizza van. She then strikes up a conversation with one of his friends who has stayed behind at the house. The brother and sister have initial physical contact only in a very compromising position—Boni is masturbating, and he leans over to grab the hair of the woman in bed with him, only to discover it is his sister (the film so blurs the lines between fantasy and reality that it is not really a surprise to see Boni stroking a "real" woman's hair). The two fight, and Nénette leaves angrily.

But the arrival of the sister inspires an interesting shift in the film. Nénette returns the next day, and now the two have a physical fight (the previous fight was verbal). She tells her brother that she is pregnant. It is obvious that she came to her brother for help, but he is initially angry. Only when his friends show up and begin to ask questions about her does he become protective. The next scene we see of the woman in the bakery is different from what we've seen thus far in the film. We see a memory of her past with her husband, when they first met, a flashback of sorts (except that the film does not really delineate past from present, any more than it does fantasy from reality); he is a sailor, she is a bartender. The film then shows us Nénette in a room of the house we haven't yet seen: the mother's bedroom, a kind of shrine to her memory, where we see pictures of her. Then we see what appear to be home movies, of Boni at the beach—Nénette's memory, perhaps, of her brother. Not only does the reunion of brother and sister inspire a shift in the film to the past, but also it introduces a representation of family history.

Boni's trajectory takes another turn when he has an encounter with the woman baker outside the neighborhood. Boni has just seen the sonogram of his sister's child and has grasped the image as if it were precious and terrifying at the same time. Early in the film, Boni went to the bakery and—in what was an obviously rehearsed scenario—asked for a nice, long baguette. The woman informs him that all of the baguettes are the same length. Boni comes across in that scene as an immature teenager deploying obvious sexual innuendo. After his relationship with his sister and her baby is redefined, so too is Boni's relationship to the woman. In what appears to be yet another fantasy, we see the woman with her husband, but also with a baby, and as one commentator on the film suggests, "the nature of the fantasy adapts itself to the changes in Boni" (Ortoli 2002: 10).

Immediately after this episode, Boni sees the woman at a store, and she invites him to have coffee with her. The scene is one of the most touching and beautifully rendered in all of Denis's work. Boni sits in stunned silence as the woman talks at great length about pheromones and the ways in which "invisible fluids" determine relationships. She extends her arm for Boni to smell and then tells him she wears no cologne so as not to interfere with the natural scent of her body (figs. 11, 12). There is a putative shot-reverse shot here, but during most of the scene, we watch the woman. One could argue that she remains the object of male fantasy here—or, conversely, that once she speaks, she

Figure 11: Boni in *Nénette and Boni* |

Figure 12: The *boulangère* in *Nénette and Boni* |

becomes decidedly less desirable (if that is how we are to interpret Boni's silence). Or one could say that once Boni has become attached to his sister's baby, the woman is less of a sexual object and more of a maternal one. In becoming "maternal" rather than "sexual," the woman thus embodies one of the oldest stereotypes about women imaginable, the mother/whore dichotomy.

But something else is happening here. The woman's discussion of "invisible fluids" is emblematic of the film itself. It is as if she were a spectator explicating what the film repeatedly demonstrates. In other words, the woman is certainly visible in terms of the competing claims of the maternal and the sexual, but there is a definite movement beyond that dichotomy in this scene in which her discussion of "invisible fluids" summarizes beautifully the film's preoccupation with flow—with water, with movement, with transformation (see Grugeau 1997). As Frédéric Strauss puts it, the "secret chemical dialogue" of which she speaks is also what Claire Denis aims to achieve in the relations between images (1997: 65).

Boni's ties to the woman are as linked to cycles of creation and transformation as they are to his sexual fantasies. Both of them work with dough (as does the woman's husband, played by Vincent Gallo; at one point he complains, as he brings a tray of croissants into the shop, about how sick he is of making croissants). Immediately after the encounter in the café, we see a round loaf of dough. Boni caresses the dough with his hands and then leans over to kiss it. The gesture could be seen as related to either the woman or his sister—sexual in the first case, protective in the second. Then Boni pounds the pizza dough (with a frenzy somewhat reminiscent of Colin's solo dance in *U.S. Go Home*), while he speaks his sexual fantasies about the bakery owner. Later events make clear that this is also a significant transitional moment in the film. When Nénette attempts to abort the child by drinking vinegar and sitting in a hot bath with mustard, Boni discovers her and holds her stomach tenderly, just as he holds the pizza dough here. Boni wants Nénette's child, and in wanting her child, he wants to reconnect with his sister. Although it sounds incredibly clichéd to say that Boni wants to become a mother, there is that element—not of taking over the mother's role, but of reconnecting to the mother he lost, and of moving from the simple objectification of women to a profound identification with them.

Grégoire Colin's performance is exquisite in these terms, for he is both an angry nineteen-year-old, who wants to find himself a good lay, and a frightened, vulnerable teenager who misses his mother and wants something in his life to fill up the hole left by her death. Denis said that before she made *U.S. Go Home,* she wanted to work with Colin after seeing him in Tonie Marshall's film, *Pas très catholique* (1993) (Adler 1997). In Marshall's film, Colin gives a stunning performance as a teenager whose mother, a private investigator, comes back into his life after having left him and his father years before. He lives with his father, a respected businessman about whom incriminating material has been discovered. Colin is a vulnerable and sweet teenager who is thrilled at seeing his mother again, but he flies into a rage when he discovers that she has incriminating material about his father. Colin erupts, but with the same vulnerability and hurt as when he is joyful at seeing his mother. One critic refers to *Nénette and Boni* as an ode to Grégoire Colin (Ortoli 2002: 6), while another praises the unique complicity between Denis and Colin in the film (Garbarz 1997: 39).

The narrative of *Nénette and Boni,* then, traces the coming together of brother and sister, with attendant changes: Boni's sexual fantasies are transformed, and his sister, and then her child, take the place of the woman in the bakery. Given how the substitution of sister/child for the woman takes place, the film does indeed raise the question if not of incest then of the sexual contours of the relationship between siblings. Recall that the first encounter between brother and sister is in bed, when Boni is masturbating. While Boni's attentions become focused on Nénette's child, we see in many of his gestures some of the same desire present in his fantasies about the woman in the bakery. But just as importantly, Boni's sexual fantasies reveal, from the outset, a preoccupation with family, another kind of desire, the desire for home, for a lost mother. The point here, however, is not to separate neatly the sexual desire from the desire for "something else," but to recognize how the film consistently reveals how different kinds of desire are strongly interconnected.

The family intrigue of the film requires, perhaps, that Nénette and Boni's father—"Monsieur Luminaire" (played by Jacques Nolot)—be literally eliminated, and once again, the question of "real" and "fake" is raised. The father's ties to some kind of criminal activity are suggested but never really specified (Boni's criminal activities are more concrete but are also presented somewhat elliptically). When the father is threatened by two thugs, it is perhaps obvious that he will die, but nonetheless the murder happens suddenly, on the street, as he and his female companion are departing in their car. The father was, in any case, an ephemeral presence in his son's eyes (he tries to defend himself to Boni by telling him that his mother lost all interest in him sexually once Boni was born, and that all she ever cared about was her son).

The film concludes as Nénette gives birth, and her brother, armed with the rifle we see at several points in the film, comes to the hospital and insists on taking the child. He brings the baby home and rubs its belly—again, in a visual echo of Boni and the bread dough. With the haunting music of the Tindersticks, the film concludes with one phrase spoken twice: "You pissed on me," says Boni to the baby, in delight and joy (fig. 13). But the last image of the film belongs to Nénette. When we see her in the hospital, a nurse attempts to waken her, and Nénette pretends to be asleep. She opens her eyes and smiles, and she has the same peaceful expression we saw when she appeared in the swimming pool at the beginning of the film. At the film's conclusion, she is outdoors, wistful, looking through an ashtray for a cigarette stub. She looks up, but it is not really possible to read any particular emotion in her face (fig. 14).

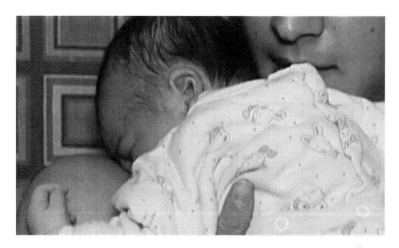

Figure 13: Boni at the conclusion of *Nénette and Boni*

Figure 14: Nénette at the conclusion of *Nénette and Boni*

The final image raises the question somewhat enigmatically of the place of Nénette in the film. Obviously she is important—her child is the catalyst for Boni's transformation. But there is something weirdly familiar about her role—the woman who functions as a means of male transformation. What saves the film from being a repetition of this motif of the woman as vehicle or catalyst is the focus on brother and sister, that is, on the reconceptualization of a family dynamic. While much about Boni suggests stereotypically masculine swagger, the film consistently shows and reveals the frightened and insecure teenager trying on different roles. The role that finally fits is that of parent—not of father, specifically, but of loving parent. If a new definition of family ties emerges in the film, it is one from which the father—that is, patriarchal authority—has been evacuated just as forcefully as the real father is eliminated. In both *U.S Go Home* and *Nénette and Boni,* the relationship between brother and sister creates a framework for a reinvention of one's self.[4] In *U.S. Go Home,* the sister's story is central, and in *Nénette and Boni,* the brother's story takes center stage. But ultimately both films focus on the brother-sister relationship as it offers a staging of the patterns of gender expectations of the traditional family, to be sure, but also the space for a reinvention of those very expectations.

Rhythms of the Night: *I Can't Sleep* and *Beau Travail*

Strangers populate the films of Claire Denis, from dislocated individuals who cross the boundaries separating past and present, to exiles who live sometimes on the margins, sometimes in the shifting spaces of the geographies of race and gender and colonization. If Denis's films are inhabited by strangers, the obvious attendant question is: strangers to whom? In some cases, the answer is obvious, particularly in those films engaged directly with the legacies of colonization and decolonization— strangers to any fixed concept of home (France in *Chocolat*), strangers because they are immigrants (Jocelyn and Dah in *No Fear, No Die*). In a more general sense, the "strangers" in Denis's films are not only characters embodied by individual actors but bodies in motion, approached as objects of wonder and curiosity. More often than not, the bodies that receive the most attention in Denis's films are the bodies of men, and these bodies are presented as "strange"—not necessarily in a pejorative sense. Although plenty of female bodies inhabit Denis's work, the male body is more consistently an object of curiosity and fascination.

Many of Denis's films can be understood as explorations of masculinity, from the bond between the two men in *No Fear, No Die* to the sexual fantasies of Boni in *Nénette and Boni*. The two films that focus most attentively on the "strange" male body are, certainly not coincidentally, also the films where homosexual and homoerotic bonds are objects of fascination. In the case of *I Can't Sleep* (1994), the fascination seems to focus on a gay man, secondarily on his lover(s); in *Beau travail* (2000), on the wide range of homoerotic connections both nurtured and repressed in the context of the French Foreign Legion. In both films, these objects of fascination are shaped and defined by a range of observers, most of whom are women. *I Can't Sleep* is the third film in the triptych that also includes *Chocolat* (colonization and decolonization) and *No Fear, No Die* (immigration); the third film "concludes," as it were, with assimilation. Like its predecessors, *I Can't Sleep* is preoccupied with what might be called the nomadic subjects of the contemporary, post-decolonization landscape, figures who move through space, settling here and there, yet always experiencing a sense of displacement.

I Can't Sleep is inspired by the case of Thierry Paulin, a young, gay, black HIV-positive man who, in the 1980s in Paris, killed nineteen elderly women, with the assistance of his lover. Paulin died in prison before he was tried for the murders. His case was the subject of obsessive media attention in France, and he was described routinely as a horrible creature. *Paris Match* ran an amply illustrated series of articles on Paulin under the title "The Monster," and the description that accompanies one of the photographs of him summarizes the kind of terror Paulin inspired, where his marginal status made him even more monstrous: "A bleach-blond mulatto, a gay drag queen and a drug addict, Thierry Paulin was the life of the party for Paris's in-crowd of outcasts" ("Le Monstre" 1987: 35). Paulin was also described by those who knew him, whether well or just slightly, as a pleasant, engaging, and charming young man.

One might well wonder what inspired Claire Denis to take on a project like this. Paulin's race and sexuality were routinely mentioned as a means of inspiring dread and horror, as if the murder of nineteen women were not enough. How, then, could one make a film inspired by the Paulin case without indulging the racism and homophobia that were part and parcel of the coverage of his case? Denis's decision was to "evacuate" from the film any notion of "political correctness," that is, to refuse to engage with the question of what can or cannot be deemed an acceptable representation of race or sexuality. "Political correctness," said Denis, "is a corollary of racism. I liked *Philadelphia* [Jonathan Demme's 1993 film about a lawyer with AIDS, played by Tom Hanks, who is fired from his law firm, and the lawyer, played by Denzel Washington, who takes on his case], but the close-up of Denzel Washington, with the accompanying music by La Callas, where one waits for a tear to appear on his face, is an insulting shot for a black actor, precisely because it belongs to the category of the 'correct'" (Jousse and Strauss 1994: 28).

Denis has described her initial approach to the film as naïve: "Is someone born a monster or does he becomes a monster?" Instead of approaching that question directly, Denis and co-screenwriter Jean-Pôl Fargeau decided "to question ourselves what it is to be the brother, or the mother, or the neighbour of a monster" (Romney 2000). The "track" chosen (her term) was based on an old French board game, the "goose game," where one follows a concentric circle from outside to inside. In the film, the city of Paris is the game board, and the initial player, as it were, is Daïga, (Katerina Golubeva), a woman from Lithuania whose arrival in the city marks the beginning of the film.[5]

I Can't Sleep is "inspired" by the Paulin case, and when the film came out, it was received as a scandalous resuscitation of the crimes. The French newspaper *France-Soir* did a cover story on the film when it appeared at the Cannes Film Festival, with the headline "Paulin, the Killer, a Star at Cannes." To be sure, the character of Camille is based on Paulin; as played by Richard Courcet, he is black, gay, HIV-positive, and a murderer. But there is no commission of a crime until an hour into the film, and then two murders are shown very quickly, one right after the other. The murders are more horrifying, perhaps, for the reticence with which they are shown. If the film scandalized, it wasn't because of the spectacle of murder, but rather because of the refusal of the film to present Camille in either/or terms, that is, as either a monster or as a victim.

The film's portrayal of Camille is perhaps best assessed in a lengthy scene that shows him performing, in drag, at a gay club (fig. 15). The song he performs, "Le lien défait" (The Untied Bond), is by Jean-Louis

Figure 15: Camille in performance in *I Can't Sleep*
(photo by Isabelle Weingarten)

Murat (who also composed the title song for the film that we hear over the closing credits). Here, as elsewhere in the film, Camille inhabits his drag persona but seems distant from it at the same time. Part of this effect is literal, since Camille does not fully conform to the cliché of a drag performer. He wears a dress, and gloves, and a band around his head, but there is no attempt to imitate a female persona. There are no high heels (or any shoes at all, for that matter). The dress slips down, and his chest, which is definitely not prosthetically enhanced, is visible; his makeup is not heavy enough to conceal his masculine features.

Yet Camille moves with grace in this long sequence. Murat's song is a haunting evocation of the fragility of human connections and desires, and Camille's performance of it is almost ethereal. I say "almost" because the performance is also emphatically one of flesh, of gravity. Numerous spectators in the club, all of them male, are seen responding to Camille in awe, but there are moments when they appear to be objects of the look as much as Camille is. In other words, in this performance the very categories upon which our notions of performance rely—the distinction between spectator and spectacle—are undone, like the undoing of the bond referred to in the title of Murat's song.

The central preoccupation of the film is the chance encounters established between a wide range of characters, three of whom are central. First, is Camille himself, whose immediate circle consists of his lover, Raphael, and another man, a doctor, on the one hand, and his family, on the other. Second, is Camille's brother Théo, who is struggling to raise his child, to reconnect with his estranged wife, and to make a return to Martinique, where he believes life will be considerably better, particularly for his son, than in Paris. Finally, is Daïga, the Lithuanian immigrant whose arrival in the city marks the beginning of the "goose game." Daïga has her own dreams of an acting career, inspired by a theater director whom she met during an acting workshop and who, it seems, promised her a job in Paris. The film begins as Daïga arrives in the city in her beat-up car and makes her way to the apartment of her great-aunt, who lives in the eighteenth arrondissement. As Daïga drives into the city, we hear, on her car radio, news reports on the continuing activities of the "granny killer," but only later do we realize that Daïga speaks little if any French, so she has no idea of what is going on. But the film intercuts Daïga's arrival with the discovery of the body of the latest victim of the serial killer. Thus a connection is made between Daïga's arrival in the city and the crimes themselves. These connections become more and more tightly woven as the film progresses. Daïga's great-aunt finds her a place to stay in a hotel run by Ninon (Line Renaud), a close friend. The hotel just happens to be where Camille and his lover reside.

Ninon adores the two young men, and as they leave the hotel one evening, she tells Daïga—right after warning her about the dangers of Paris at night—that they are sweet and kind. Denis has said that one of the intriguing factors of the Thierry Paulin case was that so many people crossed his path and interacted with him without having a clue as to his crimes. Coincidentally, one of those people was Line Renaud. She once interviewed Thierry Paulin for a stage show she was organizing, and only after his arrest did she realize that he—and she—were two of the many strangers and acquaintances who populate an urban space with no real clue about what might be happening behind closed doors or beyond public spaces (Pantel 1994: 3). Ironically, Renaud's character leads self-defense classes for elderly women in the neighborhood so they can protect themselves, while the killer is, literally, under her own roof.

Line Renaud is not only a character in the film; she provides (in a duet with Dean Martin) part of the soundtrack. When we see Daïga enter the city in her car, one of the songs we hear is "Relax-ay-voo," a song from the 1950s that seems both appropriate and out of place. The song is, as its title implies, a French-American entreaty to relax, let loose, and do things the French way (i.e., in a carefree manner). It is appropriate because it is a way of introducing Renaud, and because it provides a counterpoint to the news we hear about the killer; and it is out of place because it seems jarring in relationship to what we see, a young woman driving into the city, and to what we have just heard, "Cancion," an upbeat orchestral number that seems to frame Daïga's arrival into the city as if she were about to step into a dance. In Denis's previous work, collaboration with the musician Abdullah Ibrahim (*Chocolat* and *No Fear, No Die*) and with the group Tindersticks (*Nénette and Boni*) resulted in soundtracks that are integrally connected to the films, not "added" after the fact. *U.S. Go Home* uses music from the 1960s, and the arrangement of the music does not simply evoke the era but engages, in a complex way, with what is seen and heard on screen. While musician and singer Jean-Louis Murat did indeed collaborate on *I Can't Sleep,* the majority of the music heard in the film is from a wide array of sources.

The songs that mark Daïga's arrival create a mood, a feel, of a kind of expansiveness. Throughout the film—most notably in Camille's lip-sync of "Le lien défait," and in a scene that will be discussed below, when Théo performs with the Caribbean musician Kali the song "Racines"—music is also used to create impressions of individual characters. Daïga doesn't actually perform a song, and she is associated with a wide range of musical styles, perhaps as a kind of accompaniment to her function in the film, to investigate and to move through different layers of the city, to be a go-between among the characters. If Daïga and Line Renaud are connected by the sound of Renaud's duet when Daïga enters the city, and again when Daïga stays at Ninon's hotel, the scene that marks genuine intimacy between the two occurs when they are both drunk and listening to Procol Harum's "A Whiter Shade of Pale." The song has such a history, and is so familiar as a mournful tribute to times gone by, that its appearance in the film could be seen as a bit on the maudlin side (as Renaud's character says, she has done plenty of grinding to this song!). But Claire Denis's approach to music instead works to situate familiar songs in unfamiliar contexts, and here the song becomes a momentary connection between two women of different generations who dance together in a moment that evokes both the present and the past.

The scene in question shows the two women in the foreground of the image, while a woman of yet another generation is visible, framed in the background—Ninon's mother, who lives with her, and who is played by Line Renaud's actual mother. The woman is a potential victim of the killer (and if this were a very different kind of film, she would definitely be among the victims). During the entire scene, the old woman is intermittently visible in the background. While her function may be primarily that of, precisely, the possible next victim, she tells the two women that she cannot go to bed because she isn't sleepy—"J'ai pas sommeil," she says, in the only direct reference to the title of the film. If the title suggests, in more general terms, a nighttime atmosphere of dark streets, and perhaps of a relationship between crime and the wandering associated with insomnia, the grounding of the title in this scene offers a very different kind of association, the nightly fatigue of an old woman, whose location in the background of the image, as the observer of the dance and conversation between Ninon and Daïga, mirrors that of the spectator.

Daïga works as a maid in the hotel, and eventually her dreams of acting are shattered when she realizes that the theater director was interested in sleeping with her, not in helping her career. Throughout the film, Daïga is an observer, and she soon becomes curious about the two men in the hotel, Camille in particular. She adopts the position of a classic voyeur as she sees the two men having sex in their room; she is more of an investigator when she cleans their rooms and inspects the glamour photographs of Camille she finds there. While Camille's actions are presented as genuinely horrifying, the film brings to the surface the many ways in which people are capable of violent actions, including Daïga: driving her car one day, she happens to see the theater director in his (considerably more expensive) car, and she gleefully and exuberantly smashes into it over and over again.

This leads to yet another coincidental encounter. Daïga has to go to the police station, and there she sees drawings of Camille and his lover, the two men she recognizes from the hotel. One of their recent victims survived and was able to provide descriptions of them. Only after Daïga has seen the drawings, thus only after she knows "who" Camille is, does she take her observation of him to another level, by pursuing him on the street and standing next to him in a café. Their hands touch briefly when she asks for sugar. Shortly after this encounter, Camille is captured, yet we do not know if Daïga was instrumental in his arrest or not. (As in the real Paulin case, the murderer is stopped by police for an identity check, quite common for black and Arab men in Paris; once he is taken to the police station, his criminal identity is discovered.) We do see Daïga proceed, after her encounter with Camille in the café, to his hotel room, where she takes the money she finds, money taken from the women victims.

Daïga functions as a detective, and while she "profits" from her discovery, she appears to be driven by curiosity, by fascination. Daïga's arrival in Paris is interwoven not only with the story of Camille but also with the story of Théo, Camille's brother. As the "good son," Alex Descas deliberately played the role against type; he is taciturn, even surly at times. Denis has noted that Descas "sensed the risk of being the good brother in opposition to the bad brother, and, with good reason, he found the idea ridiculous. So he consistently defined his character as on the verge of being unpleasant and hard, and it was a good choice" (Jousse and Strauss 1994: 27). Théo is a musician and a tradesman who has a stormy relationship with his white wife (played by Béatrice Dalle). While Théo states his belief that they and their child will have a better life in Martinique, his only concrete evocation of that life is in the mocking description he provides to his wife and his mother-in-law (in response to their reluctance to see the move as positive) of a dreamy beachside existence, a tourist cliché, as if to suggest that his dreams are at best utopian, at worst, already foreclosed.

Just as Daïga's arrival and subsequent stay in Paris is shaped by the connections with Camille, so too is Daïga's situation evoked in relationship to Théo's. Both Daïga and Théo are members of marginalized communities, and both of them are outsiders—Daïga's status in this regard is marked by her lack of knowledge of the French language, and Théo's by his race. Yet Daïga, the Lithuanian who can barely speak French, can more easily "pass" as French, whereas Théo, who *is* French, is the more visible outsider. As Daïga tries to make a life in the city, Théo desperately tries to leave the city. Both characters suffer the daily indignities of gender and race. Daïga is harassed by police officers and by a man who pursues her aggressively on the street; Théo is treated condescendingly, and then viciously, by a wealthy white woman who tries to cheat him after he has built bookshelves in her apartment.

We most often see Daïga as she walks or drives; the tracking shot tracks her as she tracks Camille. Théo is associated with a different kind of cinematic space than the movement through space emphasized by the moving camera that tracks Daïga. To escape the confines of his apartment, he sleeps, with his son, on the roof of the apartment building. Noting that the scene on the roof allows a view of an illuminated, nocturnal Paris, Martine Beugnet notes as well that, particularly when Mona joins her husband and son, we have here "one of the rare moments of apparent serenity" in the film (Beugnet 2000a: 237). At several moments, we watch Théo as he gazes, from on high, at the city. Théo possesses, literally, a "long view," yet he cannot "see" his brother. The point is made emphatically when the film cuts from Théo looking out from the balcony of his apartment, to the commission of the first murder by Camille and his lover/accomplice.

The tracking shot is intimately associated with Daïga from the very beginning of the film. But another kind of shot, with an attendant different perspective, is introduced before we see Daïga. The film opens with a shot of two police officers who are laughing hysterically in a helicopter that flies over the city and its outskirts. We see a cheesy pinup image of a woman (they don't really pay attention to it, but it is placed directly in the line of vision of the spectator), which finds a visual echo, of sorts, a few moments later when two men (mirroring the two men in the helicopter) in a car pass Daïga and ogle her. It is tempting to situate this opening image of the policemen as the high-angle, long shot of authority, and the field of their vision as the establishing shot that will lead us to the overview of the city. The fact that the men are laughing doesn't assist in the creation of any kind of authority in this image, and throughout the film various police officers are presented as somewhat abusive, incompetent creatures. Curiously, it is just the kind of visual shot—the high-angle, long shot—that is associated with Théo.

It comes as little surprise that the presumably authoritative perspectives of police officers are undermined in the film. But it is surprising that as the film takes us across the shifting perspectives on the city and its inhabitants, the high-angle, long shot is dissociated from the police and associated virtually exclusively with Théo. Yet the shift is enormously suggestive of what exactly is at stake in Théo's vision: a desire for both connection and distance. The desire is linked to the wish to return to Martinique, a desire mocked by Camille and resisted by Mona, Théo's wife. If Théo spitefully describes Martinique as a "primitive paradise" to his mother-in-law, the evocation of Martinique occurs in more utopian ways elsewhere in the film. We see Théo and Camille at a birthday party for their mother, populated by family members, where Caribbean music plays and people dance joyfully. Here, a photograph of a woman—undoubtedly Camille and Théo's grandmother—serves as an evocation of Martinique as a fantasy of a remembered connection. The same photograph appears in Camille's hotel room and in Théo's apartment.

Perhaps the most interesting evocation of Martinique, now in terms more concrete than an old photograph and more complex than a tourist's cliché, occurs when Théo performs at a club, accompanying the musician Kali in a performance of "Racines." (Kali is a West Indian musician, and the song is sung partially in Creole.) Aside from the scene at his mother's birthday party, this is virtually the only time in the film when we see Théo smile (slightly). A woman seems to catch his eye, but then his gaze also seems to rest on an elderly couple dancing to the music. Camille is among the spectators at the club. This beautiful yet brief evocation of Théo's pleasure is foreclosed quickly. Kali's music continues over a tracking shot of Camille as he leaves the club and walks down the street. In a combination tracking shot/shot-reverse shot, we see two men observe him, and initially they seem gleeful. Only after their pursuit of Camille has been established is it revealed that they are police officers (figs. 16, 17, 18, 19). Camille is arrested, and the music comes abruptly to a halt. The tracking shot becomes, emphatically, a means of surveillance, and yet the accompanying music provides a haunting evocation of passage, of a movement out of the city, toward something else.

Daïga and Théo never meet in the film; their paths never cross directly. At the conclusion, after Camille has been arrested and Théo accompanies their mother and sister to the police station, we watch as Théo leaves the station and walks down the city street. He is wearing white shoes that were a peace offering from his wife. They pinched his feet, but he insisted on wearing them anyhow. One senses that Théo's dreams of movement, of a return to Martinique, have been dramatically

Figure 16: The tracking shot as surveillance in
I Can't Sleep

Figure 17: The tracking shot as surveillance in
I Can't Sleep

Figure 18: The tracking shot as surveillance in
I Can't Sleep

Figure 19: The tracking shot as surveillance in
I Can't Sleep

foreclosed, or at the very least deferred. We have no idea where Théo is going, only that he is walking in those very uncomfortable shoes. We then cut to Daïga, who is driving out of the city. We have no idea where she is going either, although following the circle of the film, one assumes she is returning to Lithuania. Daïga is, at least, on the move. The film began with her arrival in the city in the early morning hours, and it concludes with her departure at night, now with the money she took from Camille's room. Daïga wanted to stay in Paris, and Théo wanted to leave. If their dreams have been stalled, their roles are not exactly reversed. In the end, the white woman's narration—Daïga as a symmetrical frame for the film, whose discoveries match those of the film's spectator—provides closure. In a somewhat perverse sense, her curiosity has paid off—she has made some money in Paris. But we are left with the haunting sense that the price paid for her mobility is the foreclosure of the dreams of Théo. The most significant encounter of bodies in motion in the film may well be this one, realized not in the flesh but through film editing, making visible the ways in which bodies in motion are always relative.

Beau travail may well be the ultimate film about strangerhood, since members of the French Foreign Legion are strangers wherever they go. The film was conceived as a contribution to a television series on "foreign lands," produced by Pierre Chevalier and Patrick Grandperret for ARTE. Denis used the telefilm as an opportunity to consider not someone's travels to a foreign land but rather "the notion of foreignness" (Renouard and Wajeman 2001: 2). The process of thinking through the notion took Denis and her usual co-screenwriter, Jean-Pôl Fargeau, to two poems by Melville as well as his novella *Billy Budd, Sailor,* on the one hand, and to the East African country of Djibouti (where she lived as a child) and the French Foreign Legion, on the other. From the outset, the project was beset with difficulties, since not only did Denis not receive any help from officials in Djibouti (whether French or Djiboutian), but also she had to contend with a swirl of rumors about the film: "What I heard was a real shock: that I was going to make an anti-French army film, then a porn film about Legionnaires and young Ethiopian girls, and then a film about homosexuality in the Legion" (Renouard and Wajeman 2001: 5).

Denis worked with her usual collaborators on the film (Fargeau, Agnès Godard), and she also worked with choreographer Bernardo Montet, who was an integral part of the preparation of the film. In Paris before shooting started, he worked with the actors who play the Legionnaires. Denis and Fargeau also worked a bit differently from usual on the preparation of the script; Fargeau wrote Galoup's notebooks, which became, as Denis says, like a "libretto" for the film. Montet's choreography was not added on to an existing script but was, rather, essential to the conception of the film from the outset (Renouard and Wajeman 2001: 5).

The film has had a phenomenal reception, and it has been shown at more international festivals and received more commentary than any of Denis's other films. Some critics seem to have discovered Denis as a serious filmmaker on the basis of *Beau travail*.[6] Calling *I Can't Sleep* a film that offered an "interesting portrait of a Paris neighborhood" but nonetheless "wallowed in a kind of professional morbidity," and *Nénette and Boni* a "sicko story about two teenage siblings in Marseilles," Jonathan Rosenbaum asks, in his glowing review of *Beau travail*: "Did previous Denis films have a poetry I didn't notice or appreciate, or did she make a quantum leap as an artist in *Beau Travail?* Probably some of both" (2000: 4).

The preoccupations of *Beau travail* seem to me relatively consistent with Denis's earlier work; what has changed in this film is the level of abstraction, on the one hand, and the increasingly deliberate focus on the male body, on the other. As in other works by Denis, male bodies are investigated and the particular bonds between men are explored, and the complex encounters between Africa and France are central. But in *Beau travail* there is even less reliance on dialogue than in previous films, and a more emphatic reliance on bodies as they move through beautiful but desolate landscapes. If the music of Kali, in *I Can't Sleep,* conjures up the desire for Martinique, in *Beau travail* the music has much more of a counterpoint function in relationship to what is seen on screen; and if dance has always been a privileged motif in Denis's films, in *Beau travail* it is far more than a motif. Rather, the entire film functions as a kind of choreographed ritual.

There is a core narrative in *Beau travail,* one that is borrowed from Herman Melville's *Billy Budd* as well as Jean-Luc Godard's *Le Petit soldat* (1960). It draws as well on an entire tradition of the iconography of the French Foreign Legion, from Jean Gabin in *La Bandéra* (directed by Julien Duvivier, 1935) to Gary Cooper in *Beau Geste* (directed by William Wellman, 1939). Two narrative threads are particularly important. First, the triangular structure of *Billy Budd* is adapted to tell the tale of desire, envy, and jealousy. Galoup (Denis Lavant) adores Bruno Forestier (Michel Subor), the commander of his Legion outpost in Djibouti. A new recruit, Gilles Sentain (Grégoire Colin), attracts the attention of Forestier when he performs a daring rescue after a helicopter crash. Galoup immediately perceives Sentain as a threat, and Galoup jumps on an opportunity to expel Sentain from the group. When a soldier is punished by Galoup, Sentain comes to his aid. The punishment for Sentain is banishment, and it becomes a death sentence when Galoup provides Sentain with a broken compass. Yet Sentain is found by members of the Djiboutian community, who take care of him; it is unclear if he dies or survives. Galoup is then punished by expulsion from the Legion. The film unfolds, more or less, as Galoup's recollection of the drama that led to his expulsion and, we are led to believe, suicide. But never is the relationship between Galoup's memories and what "really" happened made clear. It isn't that Galoup is necessarily an "unreliable" narrator but that his narration is the very symptom the film explores.

The second narrative thread is suggested by the very first words that Galoup speaks in the film: "Marseille, end of February. I have time before me now." The second sentence cites the last words spoken by Bruno Forestier, the main character in Godard's *Le Petit soldat*: "I have time before me now." With actor Michel Subor playing Bruno Forestier more than three decades later, *Beau travail* is a kind of homage to Godard's film. In *Le Petit soldat,* Forestier is a political wanderer against the backdrop of the French Algerian War (the film was banned for a number of years because of its allusions to torture). "I told myself," says Denis, "that after the film, when he leaves the army and kills the correspondent for the FLN [Front de Libération Nationale, the Algerian independence movement], Forestier joined the French Foreign Legion" (Lalanne and Larcher 2000: 51). Subor's character is not the only homage to Godard's film, for the very structure of *Beau travail* cites the narrative device of voice-over used throughout *Le Petit soldat.* Galoup, not Forestier, becomes the literal "voice" of the film, although Denis, like Godard, does not attribute any particular authority to the voice-over. To the contrary: while we are aware in the film that Galoup is narrating the events that led to his expulsion from the Legion, the precise connections between those events are left ambiguous.

The citation of Bruno Forestier is equally a citation of the New Wave. While the two texts that inform the film, *Billy Budd* and *Le Petit soldat,* are obviously different, one could also consider the practice of citation in *Beau travail* as a reading of one text through the other and, in particular, of the homosocial and homoerotic triangle of Melville's narrative through the New Wave's (and especially Godard's) explorations of heterosexual desire, particularly insofar as the woman's place, as icon, is concerned. *Le Petit soldat* was the first film by Godard to feature Anna Karina, his wife at the time, who continued to appear in his films as a beautiful woman who becomes both a love object and a figure that encourages, to varying degrees, an examination of the very status of woman-as-icon. Similarly, the function of the heterosexual couple in New Wave cinema—embodied by Subor and Karina—is read through the homosocial bonds between men so central to *Billy Budd.*[7] After noting that "the mythic coupling of Man and Woman, a New Wave staple," is "alive and well" in the films of many contemporary French directors, Kent Jones says, in his review of *Beau travail,* that "one of the many felicities of post–New Wave cinema" is the "suggestion of cinema without a strict sexual orientation" (2000: 26). In other words, then, Subor and Bruno Forestier also bring to *Beau travail* a point of reference for an opening up of the Legion to heterosexual desire beyond the clichés of the Legionnaire—or, for that matter, of the woman's traditional place in the Legionnaire narrative, the woman who waits, or follows.

The place of women in *Beau travail*—"women are in the film for sexuality, but they aren't a part of the world of the Legionnaires" says Denis (Lalanne and Larcher 2000: 52)—is one of the most pronounced examples in the film of how abstraction both conjures up the traditional view of the Legion and repudiates it at the same time. For the women may not be a central part of the Legionnaires' world, but they are definitely part of the spectators' world. All of the women in the film are black, and they fall into two distinct categories, conjured in the beginning of the film in the contrast between the women on the dance floor and the women whom we see in the train—between, that is, women who let loose, who mug for the camera, whose dress is a combination of European and African, who dance, and women whose movements are restrained, who observe the Legionnaires (and, at the conclusion of the film, care for the near-dead Sentain), and who wear traditional garb, their heads covered. While we see both groups of women interacting with men (the first with the Legionnaires, the second with other Djiboutians), there is also a sense of a communal female identity. The women at the disco provide a sense of a female world that could be construed as liberating (sensual, full of movement, laughter) or constraining (they are the providers of pleasure for men). The more traditional women are, perhaps ironically, more defined as independent entities.

Denis has alluded to the number of prostitutes in Djibouti, but the women whom we see at the disco in this film are not coded stereotypically as prostitutes. They very definitely signify pleasure, however, and they stand in sharp contrast to the women who function as somewhat awed and perplexed observers of the Legionnaires. Yet these two groups of women share one characteristic, and that is that they function as observers within the film, witnesses. For Jonathan Rosenbaum, this is the aspect of *Beau travail* that most clearly marks the film as a film by a woman director. "Denis uses African women to subtly impose an ironic frame around the story; from beginning to end, they figure implicitly and unobtrusively as a kind of mainly mute Greek chorus—whether they're dancing in the disco, speaking in the market, appearing briefly as the girlfriends of some legionnaires (including Galoup), or serving as witnesses to part of the action" (2000: 4).

Rosenbaum's assessment is astute, and the function of women as witnesses is one that has been characteristic of almost all of Denis's work, from France, the observer of her past in *Chocolat,* to Martine, the hidden observer of Alain's frenzied dance in *U.S. Go Home,* to Daïga, the detective, of sorts, in *I Can't Sleep.* And Denis's own position as a filmmaker is one of witnessing, of observing worlds not necessarily her own. Denis's authorial signature is very much tied up in the ways in which women function as observers, yet it is also useful to see Denis's work in this context as having a lineage with that of Godard. If any single director's work has been productive in exploring the ways in which formal innovation and gender politics both inform and resist each other, and the ways in which representations of women and femininity evoke yet refuse to be contained within the polarities of a "celebration" versus a "critique" of dominant iconography, it is surely Godard's. Denis, of course, belongs to a different generation, and she brings an entirely different sensibility to the representation of gender—one in which, most notably, not all women (or men) are white. But consistently, as Claire Denis's films ask us to look, and especially to look differently at male bodies, we are asked to consider different configurations of the woman who looks.

In response to an interviewer's comment apropos of *Beau travail*, "You film men as erotic objects," Denis replied: "Not exclusively. In any case, I asked the actors to be aware of that so that we could think about it together. I was afraid of that 'erotic object' aspect of the film, tank tops, tanned skin. I wanted us to work together to maintain a distance from that. For example, filming their clothes drying on the line was a way of *de-objectifying* bodies" (Lalanne and Larcher 2000: 53). The male bodies in the film may well be masculine. Yet in their rituals of dance on the beach or in the ironing of their uniforms, they are present in such a way that the dividing lines between masculinity and femininity seem tenuous, at least insofar as male bodies are concerned. Perhaps most strikingly, the beginning of the film leads us to an unveiling of the male body, a process generally much more associated with the female body.

It is instructive, in this regard, to look at the one space in the film where male and female bodies are presented together, and that is on the dance floor of the disco. The beginning of *Beau travail* presents a series of sharply contrasting images and sounds. The film opens with a tracking shot, accompanied by the Legionnaires' song, of a wall with drawings of mountains, or cliffs, and outlines of soldiers, and what appears to be a flag. Formally, this opening tracking shot is difficult to read. Largely because of the sound track, the Legion is evoked, yet the image retains a very abstract quality. The tracking shot is ethereal and concrete at the same time. We then cut to the dance floor of the disco, to the accompaniment of Tarkan's song "Simarik," a Turkish pop song with a pulsating beat. Bodies are shot at close range, and the camera moves through the crowd of dancers on the floor, all of them African women and (mostly white) men from the Legion. The women whom we see initially introduce us to a radically different kind of space and image than the tracking shot that opens the film; they laugh, they move, and they seem to be having a genuinely good time. No single woman or single Legionnaire takes center stage, even though three main characters are introduced in this scene. While the Legionnaires are dancing, Grégoire Colin, as Gilles Sentain, walks across the dance floor as if preoccupied with something else. The camera follows him, and when he moves out of frame we are introduced to Rahel (Marta Tafesse Kassa) whom we see dancing with Galoup (Denis Lavant).

Tarkan's song is sometimes called the "kissy song" because of how its lyrics are punctuated by exaggerated sounds of loud kisses, and the scene in the disco ends with one of the soldiers mimicking the kiss, approaching but not actually kissing the woman he is dancing with. We then cut to a train station where a man, on the telephone, is saying "Djibouti." We see the interior of a train. It too is populated by both men and women, all of them African, and the women stand in sharp contrast to the women we have just seen in the disco, for they are all modestly dressed, their heads covered with scarves, and still. This is another tracking shot, thus marking a symmetry with the first shot of the film, and here we see the landscape through the window of the train. We then cut to a series of deserted objects in the landscape, and the camera then tracks once again, showing us, first, the shadows of the men and then the men themselves, moving in what is a kind of dance, and certainly a choreography of movement, although once again, in sharp contrast to the dance we see in the disco. These are solitary movements, almost physical practices of meditation. The unveiling of the men's bodies is preceded by a void, first by army artillery in disuse, and then by the shadows of the men, as if their traces precede them.

While the film observes men's bodies as they go about the rituals of dailiness, including everything from ironing to dance, visual echoes of the women that we see at the beginning scene in the disco appear throughout the film. Galoup's narration, his diary as well as his voice-over, gives the film both its substance and its ambiguity, and the passage from remembrance to fantasy is never clear. One of the recurring images in his evocation is the figure of Rahel, who is presented as Galoup's steady girlfriend, although this is not actually stated until near the conclusion of the film. Images of women, including Rahel, dancing in the disco appear at several moments in the film, seemingly part of Galoup's mental landscape of Djibouti. Rahel's function becomes more complex approximately thirty minutes into the film—before, that is, the actual events that cause Galoup's expulsion are revealed. We see Rahel, dressed very casually, without makeup, in a man's shirt—perhaps one of Galoup's—hanging up laundry to dry. Suddenly Galoup appears, in uniform, to help her. The scene suggests a dailiness to their relationship, and we see Rahel intercut with images of the Legionnaires hanging up their laundry. Then we see Galoup ironing a dark shirt (presumably the same shirt he will wear at the conclusion of the film); it isn't clear if he is in Marseille or Djibouti. As if in his mind's eye, a beautiful close-up of Rahel appears, her face suspended against the dark background.

We then see Galoup, in Djibouti, as a street vendor approaches him; Galoup buys what appears to be perfume, and we see him approach Rahel, asleep on a bed, and put the box in her hands. She doesn't awaken, but we then see a startling image of Rahel, in close-up, as she stares directly into the camera (the effect is not unlike when Anna Karina, as Nana, stares directly into the camera in Godard's *Vivre sa vie*) (fig. 20). Quickly we return to the disco, where Rahel is dancing along with the group of women, and a shot of Galoup, watching her, is inserted. It is obvious, in these brief appearances, that Rahel functions as an object of desire for Galoup, and it would be easy to see her as a stereotypical evocation of Africa as sensuality, pleasure, and comfort, and of woman as the promise of heterosexual completion. It appears as though Rahel's

Figure 20: Rahel in *Beau travail* |

function is primarily as a sexual object. Later in the film, we see Rahel in conversation with a female friend, who asks about Rahel's relationship with Galoup. The two women talk and giggle, and the sounds of their conversation continue over a shot of Galoup, as if he were in the next room listening to them.

The presentation of the two women is startlingly different from how we have seen Rahel thus far. Rahel appears in casual attire, while her friend's head is covered in a white scarf. This is the first time in the film that two kinds of women—one associated with the disco, one associated with traditional Djiboutian society—have been seen not only in the same frame but also in intimate conversation with each other. But perhaps more striking is the image in the background: a large image of the Madonna and child. Rahel's head is in symmetry with that of the Madonna, and her friend's, with the child (fig. 21). What are we to make of this sudden evocation of Rahel as a Madonna?

A partial reply is to be found in the journey of another female figure in the film, one who belongs to the more traditional category of woman. One of the first views we have of the town near where the Legionnaires are stationed occurs when we see what appears to be a completely extraneous event: a woman carrying rolled-up rugs descends from a minivan

Figure 21: Rahel and a friend in *Beau travail* |

and walks into a building. Inside the building, she converses with another woman, and they discuss the sale of a rug, made with thirteen stripes, which the woman made herself. On its own terms, this brief scene is not unlike those moments in Denis's films where a small, seemingly unrelated detail provides an evocative sense of contrast. But the woman in question, who is selling the rugs, reappears near the conclusion of the film. In the desert, a group of Djiboutians stop when they see the body of Sentain, near death, on the ground. Inside their van, this same woman appears, now to nurture Sentain back to health. This woman evokes the image of the "cosmic wet nurse" in Paul Jorion's discussion of white people in relationship to Africa (1988). Not only is she a fundamental part of the local economy, she is also, literally, a savior (figs. 22, 23). Interestingly, the film draws upon two clichéd images of Africa in the feminine—the exotic sexual being on the one hand, the nurturing traditional mother on the other—in order to complicate the opposition from within. Beneath the fantasy of the love object, Rahel, and of the woman as nurturing savior, is the common bond of the white man's absolute dependence upon the images he creates to assure him of his authority.

Beau travail concludes with the frenzied dance of Galoup on the disco floor that we have seen, intermittently, throughout the film. The dance seems both regimented and wild at the same time. If, in the previous scene, we are led to believe that Galoup is about to commit suicide, this concluding dance suggests another way to imagine the male body. There is, after all, a connection between the last two scenes. The last image we see of Galoup's body before the dance shows Galoup's arm in close-up, a vein throbbing. In the final scene, the vitality, the pulsating energy, of that detail explodes. If the film suggests, however briefly, that there are ways to imagine the breakdown of the whore/Madonna stereotype in relationship to women, no such possibility exists in relationship to Galoup. His pulsating body, whether throbbing slightly in the contemplation of suicide or performing frenetically on the dance floor, cannot escape the dualities of regimentation and desire, duty and passion.[8]

Denis's collaboration with cinematographer Agnès Godard has created a particular style of representing bodies in motion. The tracking shot is visible in virtually all of the films where they have collaborated (which means practically every film directed by Denis). In *Chocolat*, the transition from present to past is made on the road, as the camera

Figure 22: The Djiboutian woman in *Beau travail* |

Figure 23: The Djiboutian woman in *Beau travail* |

shifts from the adult France in a car moving down the highway to her as a child, sitting on the back of the family truck with Protée, observing the passing landscape. In *Nénette and Boni,* our first introduction to Boni occurs inside a rapidly moving car. In classic, traditional terms, the tracking shot is literally a shot "on track," that is, where the camera moves, but on a fixed support. (Interestingly, the French term—*le travelling*—emphasizes the effect more than the literal support.) In Denis's films, the tracking shot is far more complex, for it often moves "off track," as it were, veering wildly (as in the car with Boni). Usually the tracking shot implies a kind of measured distance, and we see plenty of such images in Denis's films, particularly in the passage of trains or cars through landscape or cityscape. But just as frequently, the tracking shot is used at close range, sometimes (as in *No Fear, No Die*) created by a handheld (or shoulder-held) camera, and sometimes as a way of capturing the fleeting connections between strangers (as in the opening of *Nénette and Boni* when the con man tries to sell counterfeit telephone cards).

Now one could say that the tracking shot loses any particular meaning when it is defined in such a loose way. Isn't it enough to say that the camera moves in Claire Denis's films? That her films provide, through intricate, sometimes dizzying camera movement, superbly complex variations on the *plan-séquence,* the single shot in which comings and goings are recorded in constant shifting cinematic space? Put another way, is the insistence on the tracking shot a mere formality, in both senses of the term? The tracking shot is not necessarily the most important element of cinematic writing in Denis's work, but in these two films, it has a particular function having to do, precisely, with the dynamics of witnessing, of "strangerhood," and of French film history.

The tracking shot inspired Jean-Luc Godard's famous declaration that the tracking shot (his specific point of reference is Alain Resnais and Marguerite Duras's 1959 film *Hiroshima mon amour*) is a "question of morality." Tracking shots call attention to the very fact of the cinema, to traveling, to moving through the world. In response to Eric Rohmer's comment that one can admire *Hiroshima mon amour* and still find it jarring in places, and to Jacques Doniol-Valcrozes's query whether this discomfort is "moral or aesthetic," Godard replied: "It's the same thing."

Tracking shots are a question of morality" (Domarchi et al. 1959; rpt. 1985: 62). More relevant, perhaps, to the tracking shot in Denis's work is Jacques Rivette's pointed criticism of a film by Gillo Pontecorvo, *Kapo,* in which a woman commits suicide in a concentration camp, and the film tracks forward to show the dead body and to isolate an extended hand as a kind of aesthetic flourish. "The man who decided to compose this forward tracking shot," writes Rivette, "deserves nothing but contempt" (1961: 55).

Both of these observations—one in which the tracking shot is praised, the other in which it is condemned—are part of the project of rethinking the cinema so central to the New Wave. Throughout the decades since the late 1950s and early 1960s, this rethinking of the cinema has been given a variety of names and definitions—the politics of form, cinematic *écriture*, political formalism, and, more recently, the politics of location.

The tracking shot has come to stand emblematically as the intersection of the physical presence of the camera and the notion of some kind of position, conscious or unconscious, a place for the spectator. Interestingly, Denis commented on the tracking shot by saying that "for me, the morality of the tracking shot has to be shared with the actor, so that the person interpreting the role be free in relationship to the fiction. There is always an element of 'and as for him . . .'" (Jousse part 3). Denis has often spoken of the close relationship she develops with actors, of the "solidarity" she regards as an ideal relationship between director and actor. Of course, this particular relationship does not apply only to the tracking shot, but the tracking shot has come to stand for a particular fact of cinema, the fact of moving through space, of creating a mobile vision in which the director's view is concrete, visible. The tracking shot in these two films reveals "strangers" to be figures in a shifting landscape, and ultimately, of course, that shifting movement becomes a figure of identification for the spectator. In *I Can't Sleep,* the tracking shot that shows the policemen following Camille has a haunting, breathtaking moment when the reverse shot reveals these figures of authority as "tracked" themselves; for a moment they seem to be reflections of the spectators at Camille's drag performance. The risk and the pleasure of "tracking strangers" in Claire Denis's films are that sooner or later we no longer know who is a stranger, or to whom.

Troubles in Paradise: *Trouble Every Day* and *Friday Night*

Claire Denis's most recent films focus more emphatically than any of her other works on the dynamics of heterosexual desire. Both of these films are very romantic, even *Trouble Every Day* (2001), which has achieved the status of Denis's most controversial work to date. Certainly we have seen, in Denis's other work, attention to the ways in which men and women desire each other, but more frequently those desires are situated in large frameworks where the love connections between men and women are but one element. In these two films, sexuality itself is center stage. All of Denis's films are about desire, but in these two films the heterosexual encounter is explored as it shapes and defines the bodies of men and women. In both films, as well, the city of Paris functions as a central element, and it is perhaps no coincidence that the only other film by Denis so defined within the city of Paris (*I Can't Sleep*) is also a film very much preoccupied with sexuality.

Trouble Every Day tells the story of two couples, whose stories are intercut throughout the film. Léo (Alex Descas) is a scientist and physician whose wife, Coré (Béatrice Dalle), suffers from a bizarre ailment. Early in the film, our first view of Coré would lead us to think she is a prostitute, as she picks up a truck driver in the desolate outskirts of the city. Later, Léo comes to find Coré. The man whom she met is not only dead but mutilated, and Coré is covered with blood. She rocks and mumbles as Léo caresses her. We are introduced to June (Tricia Vessey) and Shane Brown (Vincent Gallo, who is once again "Mr. Brown," as he was as the GI in *U.S. Go Home*) in an airplane. They are flying to Paris for their honeymoon. When Shane goes to the restroom, he has a vision of his wife covered in blood, although the look on her face is strangely blissful.

While the details are never made explicit, there is some kind of blood connection between Coré and Shane. Coré's affliction is apparent from the outset, and Shane seems to be in the earlier stages of a similar state, although by the conclusion of the film he too shows the manifestations of the affliction in terms just as horrifying as Coré's. The film continues to move back and forth between the two couples, and gradually we learn that Shane and Léo used to work together, and that Shane most likely stole Léo's controversial research concerning the effects of plants on human behavior. Whatever Shane and Coré have, it appears to have been contracted in Guyana, during a research mission led by Léo to explore the healing properties of plants.

We also learn that Léo has become an outcast in the scientific community. In Paris, Shane tries repeatedly to contact Léo at the laboratory where he (Léo) used to work, with no luck. Eventually a sympathetic woman who works there gives Shane Léo's phone number and address, and she tells him that Coré is very sick. Given how the film moves back and forth between the two couples, one expects the encounter between Shane and Léo to be cataclysmic when it finally happens. An encounter does occur, but when Shane finally goes to Léo and Coré's house, Coré is there alone. Twice previously in the film, we have seen the effects of Coré's affliction. Right before Shane arrives, Coré has devoured a male victim, the second such scene that we witness.

From the beginning of the film, we see two neighborhood teenagers who are obsessed with getting inside the house, and the fact that Coré is locked in, and manages occasionally to peer out, only heightens their determination. Finally the two young men get into the house, and one of them—very much at Coré's instigation—rips open the boards that close off her room. The sex act shifts—loudly—into a frenzy of biting, ripping, and almost playful tapping of the folds of flesh that Coré has bitten from the young man. The scene is shot at very close range, and in the dark, both of which heighten the sense of the forbidden and the mysterious. But the sounds, the guttural screams of the young man and the excited cries of Coré, make clear what is happening.

When Shane finds Coré, she is covered with blood and in something of a daze. They embrace (the suggestion was made that they were lovers during the time spent in Guyana, and perhaps whatever affliction they suffer was sexually transmitted). Coré sets fire to the house, and Shane leaves; Léo returns shortly after to find his wife dead and his home ruined.

When Shane returns to the hotel, he begins his own hunt. Just as the neighborhood teenagers were fascinated with Coré, Shane is drawn to Christelle (Florence Loiret-Caille), a maid in the hotel where Shane and June are staying. The attraction appears to work both ways; at the very least, Christelle is curious about Shane. He descends to the basement of the hotel where the lockers and changing rooms for the staff are located.

The maid is changing, getting ready to go home. When Shane embraces her, she seems to be a willing participant, but very quickly things change. He acquires a force, a desperation, and he pins her to the floor. She too begins to scream, particularly when Shane's head moves down her body and he performs oral sex on her. When he raises his head, he is covered with blood. Christelle's screams soon end, and she dies. After it is made clear that Shane is most likely headed for the same kind of fate that befell Coré, and that he is undoubtedly no longer in control of his condition, the film concludes somewhat elliptically. Shane returns to the room to take a shower, and June comes into the bathroom. He tells her that he wants to go home, and she agrees. A single droplet of blood trickles down the shower curtain, as if to suggest that no matter how much he tries, there will always be a trace of his condition and his actions.

To say that *Trouble Every Day* was controversial is an understatement (see Met [2003]). Although the film was defended by some critics, it was regarded as a pointless exercise in violence by others. Three scenes were singled out for particular scrutiny and condemnation. When Shane begins to make love to his wife in their hotel room, he stops abruptly (to protect her from his violent desire) and goes into the bathroom where he masturbates. The film shows his sperm as it jets over the sink. Shortly thereafter, June touches the sperm as if it represents a precious connection to the husband whose behavior she cannot comprehend.

The two scenes that show, in the flesh, the effects of the disease—the seduction and murder of the young man from the neighborhood and of the hotel maid—were particularly singled out as gratuitous, excessive, and/or gory. The reviewer for *Le Monde* "dedicated" its review of the film to the two women who passed out during the film at the Cannes Film Festival (Sotinel 2001). A British newspaper began its review with this sentence: "A leading French film director insisted yesterday that a movie showing brutal sex scenes, cannibalism and close-ups of ejaculation was neither controversial nor shocking" (Alberge 2001). (For the record, there is a lot of biting in the film, but no cannibalism.) Stephen Holden's review of the film is almost generous, compared to most American reviews in particular; he described *Trouble Every Day* as a "daring, intermittently beautiful failure of a movie" (2002).

A potentially troubling aspect of the film has rarely, if ever, been addressed in commentaries on the film. When a contemporary film explores the relationship between sexual desire and death, with such an emphasis on blood as the symptom as well as the sign of that connection, it is difficult *not* to see the film as related in some ways to the AIDS epidemic. *Trouble Every Day* doesn't just suggest a large, vague connection between sex and death. We are led to believe that Coré and June contracted their ailment in Guyana, and one element of discourses about AIDS is that the disease originated "somewhere else"—in Africa or in Haiti, that is, far away (ideologically if not geographically) from Europe or North America. I believe that *Trouble Every Day* subtly but forcefully undermines many of the myths about AIDS. The deadly desire has virtually nothing to do with homosexuality in the film. And the curiosity and greed of the white, heterosexual man (Shane) is at the origin of the affliction. As "Mr. Brown," Gallo's American GI from *U.S. Go Home* has become a more contemporary icon of an American man, now a greedy scientist instead of a soldier.

While many critics responded to the film as if it were a departure for Claire Denis, the film was in the planning stages for many years ahead of its making. When Denis met Vincent Gallo (during the filming of *Keep it for Yourself*, 1991), she was eager to make a film that would focus on his somewhat unusual persona—a haunting intensity, a kind of looming presence. Denis and Fargeau began working on a script, and James Schamus, of Good Machine (the producers of *Keep It for Yourself*), proposed that Denis participate in a series of six horror films made by independent, auteurist directors. Denis at first was tempted by the offer, but she soon was concerned about a danger in the project: "I sensed the risk of irony in the project, a tendency towards pastiche, which I cannot stand" (Frodon 2001). Given that "postmodernism" is a term indiscriminately attached to any artist whose work resists established categories of form, it is important to underline Denis's resistance to irony. There is certainly a strong element of detachment in Claire Denis's work, but it is not detachment in the sense of a mocking distance from the cinema, the actors, or the audience; rather, it is the kind of detachment associated with a patient, enthralled witnessing. Denis sensed that there might be the tendency, when independent directors approach genre cinema, to mock or parody the genre, and this was not what she wanted to do. Eventually Denis and Olivier Assayas conceived of a film that takes place in a hotel; the film would be divided into three parts, each directed by a different filmmaker (Atom Egoyan would have been the third). That film never came to fruition, but Assayas's contribution became *Irma Vep* (1996) and Denis's, *Trouble Every Day* (Frodon 2001).

Denis has cited a rather large group of influences on the film, aside from the desire to make a film centered on Gallo's screen persona: the photographs of Canadian Jeff Wall, with their strange evocations of familiar yet wild urban spaces; the writings of Sheridan Le Fanu; the legends of vampires, whether in film or in literature; childhood stories about monsters; African stories about half-human, half-panther creatures; and a series of films ranging from Jacques Tourneur's *Cat People* (1942) to Abel Ferrara's *The Addiction* (1995) and Brian De Palma's *Dressed to Kill* (1980) (Azoury 2001; Denis and Godard 2001; Frois and Borde 2001; Péron 2000: 16). All of these sources and inspirations share a common preoccupation with two intertwined themes about two kinds of anxiety: the unsettling anxiety that can emanate from everyday situations, and the anxieties associated with sexuality, particularly insofar as violence, pleasure, and satisfaction are concerned. Put another way, *Trouble Every Day* explores the ways in which pleasure and danger are intertwined in the realm of everyday experience.

Like many of the stories that inspired it, and the vampire tradition in particular, *Trouble Every Day* shows how various forms of science and research attempt to contain the very object they are presumably interested in exploring. The representation of science occurs largely in the laboratory where Léo used to work, and where Shane goes to find answers to the causes of and cures for his condition. The laboratory is antiseptically white, from the walls to the lab coats worn by its inhabitants, all bathed in a bright, harsh light. Brains are sliced, poked, and classified. Although the fact that Léo is black is never mentioned specifically, the visual contrast between his dark skin and the blinding whiteness of the laboratory suggests that color functions metaphorically, and that the banishment of Léo from the scientific community is also a banishment of the very difference he embodies.

Elsewhere in the film the color red is frighteningly on display, gushing, as in Shane's fantasy in the airplane of his wife dripping in blood, or smeared on the walls after Coré's experience with the intruder. In the laboratory, the color red is safely contained in the lids of samples that are stored in glass cases. But is the color red so under control after all? Throughout *Trouble Every Day,* one has that pervasive sense of anxiety, of something about to happen, of a disturbance in our fields of sound and vision. One of the repeated images and sounds associated with the laboratory is the spinning of capsules in glass containers. They make a regular, clicking noise, and they provide a visual image that suggests, at once, a controlled, regulated movement but also a vibration, a hum that is not necessarily contained by the laboratory. The capsules pulsate, exceeding both the whiteness of the laboratory and its rules and regulations concerning research and discovery.

Indeed, virtually every space represented in *Trouble Every Day* pulsates in one way or another. Calm and tranquility are underscored by a sense of foreboding. The house where Léo and Coré live creaks, and the more Léo tries to keep his wife protected, the greater energy she expends in attempting to break loose, and the greater energy the neighborhood teenagers expend in trying to get inside. The airplane where we first see Shane and June seems streamlined and orderly, until Shane goes inside a restroom and his violent images of June fill his, and our, awareness. The fashionable hotel where Shane and June stay on their honeymoon has its own dark side, the basement where employees change their clothes, wash, and hide the small treasures—lotion, soap, jam—they steal. Shane is very much drawn to that space.

This representation of pulsating spaces needs to be situated within the attention to liminal spaces so central to the film. The airplane seems to be a relatively safe and secure space, and Shane and June conform to a fairly stereotypical image of a couple on their honeymoon. When they look out the window, they see a very orderly pattern of lights (the city of Denver, Shane says). But that sense of order and security is quickly violated when Shane seeks refuge in the airplane's bathroom and experiences the vision of his wife, covered with blood, potentially, it would seem, as his victim. Initially, Léo and Coré's house seems to be a refuge from the brutal desires that are set loose when Coré ventures outside. But soon the house seems both familiar and strange. Familiar routines take place in the house—the two awaken, and Léo smokes and drinks coffee in the kitchen (fig. 24). But the house cannot sustain its function as a refuge, and quickly the boundaries between it and the outdoors become tenuous. Even within the house, a strange tension

Figure 24: Léo in *Trouble Every Day* |

exists between upstairs (where the bedroom is located) and downstairs (where the kitchen and Léo's own laboratory are situated), as if there were an invisible boundary line between rationality and desire. When we see Coré, bloodstained, on the stairway—that is, on the threshold separating upstairs from downstairs—it is clear that the boundary line has been transgressed.

The film moves quickly, in its opening scenes, from seemingly picture-perfect postcard scenes of the Seine and its bridges to the desolate landscape where Coré chooses her victim. The apparent contrast between this beautiful and recognizable image of Paris, on the one hand, and the no-man's-land of the sexual encounter, on the other, is a bit undone by the strange colors—mauve and black—that we see in the images of Paris. And throughout the opening images, we hear the haunting music of the title song by the Tindersticks. Their music itself is liminal, in that on one level it can sound quite sweet and romantic, until one becomes entranced by the rhythm of their music (and the rhythm is virtually impossible to resist), and then on another level it is haunting, pulsating in its own way, suggesting pleasure and sadness at the same time. Their music seems both to accompany the image on screen and to suggest a pull in another direction.

If the space where Coré finds her prey is suggestive of a space sharply in contrast to the views of the Seine and its bridges, the film consistently engages with the sense of a familiar place undone or rendered strange by its pulsations, its hums, its visual contours that suggest a pull toward someplace else. Coré and Léo live in a house that appears to be in the Parisian suburbs, but devoid of any particular landmarks, it is hard to say. We know only that Léo leaves and returns home on a motorcycle, and that Shane has to take a cab to get there. Shane and June, however, arrive at a respectable Parisian hotel, where the staff speaks English and the rooms are comfortably appointed. The maid is called to carry the couple's luggage to their room. We track her as she walks down the hallway, the nape of her neck the focus of our attention, as well as Shane's. She is aware of him watching her, and there is a connection suggested between them. The bed in the room has not yet been made, and Shane and June sit down on it and begin to kiss as the maid attempts to make the bed. It is an odd scene, and it is made stranger by the fact that June suddenly stands up and helps her make up the bed, as if she becomes suddenly aware that there is, indeed, another person in the room.

The corridor reappears four more times in the film, each time defined by the maid's movements and an odd relationship that she develops with the room. We watch the maid, again from behind, with the nape of her neck the center of the image, as she walks down an empty corridor and stares at the "do not disturb" sign on the door of the Browns' room. The absence of the couple—of Shane in particular—underscores a pervasive presence, as if the maid is acutely aware of their relationship, and as if Shane is tracking her down the hallway. Later in the film, the hallway is busier with activity, as several maids are going about their work. June leaves the hotel room alone, dressed in a pink suit with a black hood. She looks a bit like a fashionable Little Red Riding Hood, and here, as is always the case in the film, she is the picture of innocence. June says hello to the maid, first in English, then in French, and reaches out to touch her. The maid is friendly to her but looks on, perplexed, once June has exited the hallway. Another time, the maid finds herself in the room when Shane enters, and the look on her face suggests both anxiety and curiosity. Our final image of the maid in the hallway occurs when she seems, somewhat flagrantly, to assert her curiosity. She goes into the room and sits on the Browns' bed and smokes, as if she is enjoying the opportunity to invade their space. She doesn't smooth the bed down when she leaves, and when Shane returns, he buries his face in the indentation of her body on the bedspread. Soon, he finds her in the basement, and her curiosity coupled with his desire lead to her violent death.

Trouble Every Day explores the connection between desire and violence, and desire is, quite literally, a deadly force in the film. This may well be the most explicit way in which the film creates a liminal space, by occupying the space and time between the sparking of desire and its movement toward destruction. When the two attacks occur, it is as if there is an explosion, an outburst. But nothing is resolved as a result of these cataclysmic encounters; rather, the anxiety of everyday life, and of sexual desire, continues. Also related to this chain of desire, and to the exploration of the boundary between pleasure and danger, is a series of fantasies about birth and rebirth. When Shane has the vision of his wife covered in blood while they are traveling from the United States to Paris, the image may well be frightening, but it is more than that. In the fantasy, June is smiling, almost blissful. Given her childlike features and her innocence throughout the film, the image is equally suggestive of birth, of a child-adult being born into a frightening yet appealing world of fluids, of saturation. That June is so resolutely childlike only reemphasizes the troubled connections between desire and birth. Similarly, when Shane attacks the maid in the hotel, the sexual act is entirely different from what we see with Coré and the young man. If both sexual assaults are oral, Coré's is focused on the young man's face, his throat, and the attendant mixture of screams of pain and pleasure. Shane's is a genital attack, as if he too seeks not only oral sex but a rebirth, a reidentification with the woman as mother.

The hotel corridor is the most consistently recurring image of a liminal space in the film, and every time we see the maid walk down the hallway, it is as if there are rhythms and sounds just beneath the surface. When she makes her boldest incursion in the room, she sits on the bed and smokes. One of the details of the setting makes for an interesting connection between her and the married couple. Over the lamp, there is a scarf portraying Mona Lisa—one of those little details one assumes that June has added to the room to make it either homier or more "Parisian" (fig. 25). The scarf is green, and it serves as a visual link to an earlier scene in which the city of Paris provides a beautiful yet somewhat unsettling background for Shane and June's relationship.

As I've noted, images of Paris in the film consist both of recognizable

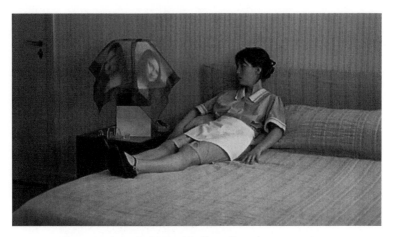

Figure 25: Laurelle in *Trouble Every Day*

images of the city, as in the opening shots of the Seine and the bridges, and unidentifiable locales, particularly the various open spaces where Coré's desires are pursued. One of the most recognizable images of Paris is the Notre Dame cathedral, and a brief interlude takes us there as Shane and June have one of their few playful moments in the film as husband and wife. We see the front of the church, and then we see the couple on one of the turrets, surrounded by gargoyles. Shane does an imitation of a monster on the move—it could be Quasimodo from any one of many adaptations of Victor Hugo's *Notre Dame de Paris,* or Frankenstein from an equally numerous group of adaptations of Mary Shelley's novel. We see Shane and June in shot-reverse shot, and for these brief moments, they could be any young couple in love in Paris (figs. 26, 27). June is wearing a bright green scarf, and as she moves to take it off, it slips out of her hands and begins to float across the rooftops of the city (fig. 28). The young couple in love is no longer the focus of the camera, but rather this floating object becomes the center of our attention. As the scarf moves, the images offer larger and larger views of the city of Paris, moving from Notre Dame to the rooftops of the neighboring buildings. The image is postcard-perfect, evoking romantic views of Paris's famous rooftops. Yet while the movements of the scarf as captured in the film are beautiful, they are also intrusive, at least in terms of the particular image of the city that is being evoked

Figure 26: Shane at Notre Dame in *Trouble Every Day*

Figure 27: June at Notre Dame in *Trouble Every Day*

Figure 28: The scarf and the rooftops of Paris in
Trouble Every Day

here. Indeed, this seemingly idyllic passage in the film may well be far more evocative of Robert Bresson's film *A Gentle Creature* (1969) than of other more romantic views of the city. At the beginning of Bresson's film, a red scarf makes a much smaller movement, as it floats down the side of an apartment building. The camera follows it and in so doing is tracing both absence and presence: a young woman has just committed suicide, and the scarf is the one last moving object associated with her body. It too is a beautiful image, but one that is unsettling. If traces of the scarf in *A Gentle Creature* remain in *Trouble Every Day,* it is to suggest the loss and absence that exist alongside the couple's happy interlude.

The function of Paris in *Trouble Every Day* is beautifully evoked in this scene. While we are observing one of the most famous and beautiful landmarks of the city, we are always reminded of forces that lie just beneath the surface. Charles Mudede has suggested that the vision of the city in Denis's film needs to be seen in relationship to how Paris was imagined, through the perspective of the nineteenth century, as a "dream city." Noting that "what is disturbing about this film . . . is the fact that it is about a nightmare that essentially has no dreamer," he says: "Walter Benjamin's, Charles Baudelaire's, Edgar Allan Poe's nineteenth-century nightmares had dreamers who could awake and dialectically restore sanity. The sinister cluster of nineteenth-century horror narratives in

Trouble Every Day seems to be activated by an alien energy source within the nightmare rather than the body of a sleeping man or woman" (2002: 2).

Historically, the zone is the name given to the part of Paris lying beyond the city proper, neither completely part of nor completely separate from the city proper. In the nineteenth and early twentieth centuries, it always connoted a wild space, both a space connected to the city and a space for the projection of various fears and anxieties about urban life. In ways that are relevant to Denis's film, the zone has been evoked in a range of films to suggest, precisely, a space that is in-between, from Louis Feuillade's exploration of the city as a dreamscape in his serial films of the second decade of the twentieth century, such as *Fantômas* and *Les Vampires,* to Jean Cocteau's concrete evocation of the zone, in *Orpheus* (1949), as the space both beneath and beyond the city, where death as well as artistic creation reside (see Callahan 1996). If the zone has a particular cinematic resonance, it is because it corresponds to the ability of cinema to be, simultaneously, the art of the real, of the everyday, as well as the art of the fantastic. Understood as a "zone," the cinema evokes both the impulse toward a realistic representation of urban space and a fantastic exploration of what lies beneath and beyond its concrete surfaces. *Trouble Every Day* takes a place alongside those films in which the zone is a central figure of both the cinema and its fictions.

At first sight, *Friday Night* (2002) would seem to have only the city of Paris in common with *Trouble Every Day*. Although I have suggested that films that appear initially to be a departure in Denis's work (such as *No Fear, No Die* and *Trouble Every Day*) are far more connected to than they are distant from her other films, *Friday Night* does, I think, represent a departure for Denis. While she did indeed "adapt" Herman Melville in *Beau travail,* never has Denis followed a literary text so closely in a film. There are elements in *Friday Night* that we have never seen before in a Denis film, from the use of dissolves to create subjectivity, to the use of playful animation to imagine the lettering on a car. Denis's recent films seem to be tracing a movement "toward Paris." While *Friday Night* has little of the dread and anxiety that characterizes *Trouble Every Day,* and it is a resolutely sunny film by the standards of Denis's other work, it nonetheless explores the desires and movements that lie beneath both the city and a woman's consciousness.

What is strikingly different about *Friday Night* is that it is concerned exclusively with the perceptions of a female protagonist. There is indeed anxiety in this film, but it is a far more pleasurable anxiety than what is evident in *Trouble Every Day*. Based on a 1998 novel by Emmanuèle Bernheim, *Friday Night* was cowritten by Denis and the author (hence the film is a departure as well from Denis's usual collaboration with Jean-Pôl Fargeau). Denis has stressed that she wanted to remain as close to the novel as possible: "'Emmanuèle kept telling me to be free with her book,' says Denis. 'But I said no, the space between the lines is too important. The rhythm and the pace of it must be reproduced. And little by little I realised the book was full of music" (James 2003: 8).

Bernheim and Denis had paired to work on the screenplay for another project, which wasn't working out quite the way Denis had hoped. When she told Bernheim this, the writer asked her what kind of story she wanted to do. "I told her what I really wanted was a story that took place today, over a short period of time, between a man and a woman. She said, 'It's funny, because I am finishing a novel where this is my subject'" (Kipp 2003: 39). The novel was *Vendredi soir.* Denis and Bernheim may work in different artistic forms, but Bernheim has written for *Cahiers du Cinéma,* and in addition to her novels, she has cowritten the screenplays for two films directed by François Ozon, *Under the Sand* (2000) and *The Swimming Pool* (2003). It is a cliché to say of a writer that she has a "cinematic imagination," but the description does fit Bernheim. Additionally, and perhaps more important in terms of the affinity between her and Denis, Bernheim draws attention to the small, concrete details of everyday life.

Bernheim's novel takes place in Paris during the transit strike in the winter of 1995. Laure is leaving her apartment to move in with her boyfriend, François, and the novel begins as she is surrounded by boxes, making last-minute arrangements before the movers come at eight o'clock the next morning. Laure is in a transitional state, moving not only from one apartment to another but from one state of being (single) to another (coupled and living together). In various ways and through various permutations, the novel explores this state of transition. It is an anxiety-ridden state in some ways: we see Laure as losing part of herself, through tiny details, such as the fact that she is selling her own car because her boyfriend's is more comfortable (she'll take the subway to work), or that she doesn't really feel comfortable calling him because he wouldn't like to be interrupted during the dinner he is attending. The first dramatic manifestation of this anxiety occurs when Laure gets into her car to leave for the evening; a man knocks at her window, and she is terrified. She locks the doors and drives away as quickly as possible. She sees in her rearview mirror that the man appears to continue to approach her. When she pulls away, relieved that he hasn't approached her again, she sees that he has gotten into the car behind her. He smiles at her.

Laure has plans to have dinner with friends, and only after she leaves her apartment and is driving does she realize that a huge transit strike is going on. She listens to the radio in the car. A newscaster encourages drivers to offer rides to those who might need one or a temporary warm place (this corresponds to what happened in 1995; in addition to the transit strike, the weather was very cold, and people were encouraged to offer rides to others). She suddenly realizes that the man who approached her was looking for a ride, not trying to do her harm, and she concludes that he smiled at her in order to mock her. Eventually Laure notices a man standing alone on the street. She sees him looking across the street, as if looking for someone—a woman, Laure presumes—whom he had arranged to meet. The man approaches Laure's car and gets in. Thus begins Laure's Friday night adventure. Laure is attracted to the man, initially because of his smell—the mixture of his leather coat, his cologne (which, she notes to herself, would smell entirely different on François), and, in particular, tobacco (Laure had quit smoking when she moved into her apartment with six flights of stairs to climb and no elevator).

The transit strike forces the inhabitants of Paris to live differently. While a radio announcer may well encourage drivers to offer rides to pedestrians, the sight of men approaching cars driven by women none-theless conjures up scenes of sexual assault or at the very least sexual danger. Indeed, this is Laure's first reaction when the man approaches her car. When Frédéric gets in her car, Laure is in, perhaps, a quite different space, literally and figuratively. The space of her car becomes an enclosure, a protection, against the potential anxiety of changing one's way of life; yet it is also a very new kind of space, one that allows Laure to navigate the public sphere of Paris in a radically different way.

The strike, the traffic jam, and Laure's car engage a different way of being, a different way of looking. All around her Laure sees evidence of the frustration caused by the traffic jam, but she becomes almost serene. Moving through the streets of Paris, she begins to move through an imaginary space, so that movement itself signifies transition, certainly, but also an activity with no purpose, no goal. Laure imagines scenarios of the man's life, from an image of the woman who must certainly be waiting for him (in an apartment, since she was not waiting on the street), to what kind of things must have happened to him when he was a taxi driver (one of the only pieces of information about him that Laure learns). Gradually she settles into a state of pure sensation, although moments of anxiety do erupt.

At one moment, Laure becomes panicked when the man takes over driving her car (he drives very fast). She asks him to stop, and he exits the car. She quickly changes her mind and begins to pursue him. She finds him in a café, and intimacy ensues—they kiss, they go to a hotel, they have dinner, they have sex. In the course of the novel, something changes in Laure, related to the way that she begins to occupy the moment, to experience sensation. Instead of imagining how others—a woman stuck in the car next to hers, Frédéric, her boyfriend François—see her, she becomes totally engaged in the experience, in the physical and sexual connection with this man. This doesn't mean that she is always immersed in the present, since she does briefly imagine that she and the man might live together. Ultimately, however, Laure leaves the hotel room in the early morning and takes a taxi to her apartment, where the movers are expected at eight o'clock. She decides that she'll tell her boyfriend that her car was stolen. In the final lines of the novel, Laure imagines that she'll meet Frédéric again. But the last sentence of the novel suggests, rather, the transformation Laure has undergone, into someone aware of herself as an autonomous being rather than as the object of someone else's fantasy. "She stretched out her legs and closed her eyes. And, with the palm of her hand, she smoothed her red skirt against her thighs" (Bernheim 1998: 110).

Denis and Bernheim have described their approach to the screenplay as a literal rendering of the novel, with some small changes (Frédéric becomes Jean, for example; we know even less about the boyfriend and about Jean in the film than we do in the novel; the red skirt that Laure takes out of a box in her car and puts on is only briefly alluded to). Initially Denis thought about the use of a voice-over, but she soon discarded the idea; the film "could not be 'once upon a time,' it has to be 'now,'" she said (Jones and Denis 2003). Although the film does follow the novel closely, it can be misleading to describe any film as a "literal" adaptation of a novel. The novel is written in a free indirect style, a mode of narration that is neither pure first person nor pure third person but which uses the third person to suggest the perspective of a first person. For example, early in the novel, we read this passage to which I alluded earlier, about Laure and her car: "She shouldn't have gone that way. Traffic was completely stalled. Laure shrugged her shoulders. She wasn't in a hurry to get to Bernard and Marie's. And this traffic jam allowed her to enjoy her car. Next week, she would get rid of it. Why keep it? François's car was much faster and more comfortable. Laure would go to work on the subway. From François's place, it was direct" (13). The novel is both inside and outside Laure's consciousness at the same time; she is observed, but she is also the subjective center of the novel. The novel works through the implications of free indirect style for a female protagonist. The doubled quality of the narration consistently juxtaposes Laure's status as subject (her thoughts are central) and as object (her thoughts and observations are represented from the outside).

Given how much cinema has relied on the objectification of women, and how the representation of a woman's subjectivity in film involves her "looks," in both senses of the term, the shift in Laure's consciousness from the novel to the film is more complicated than it might appear. In Bernheim's novel, we know very little about Laure's appearance, except that she does indeed imagine other women as more attractive than she is. After Laure gets out of the car to make a phone call, she panics when she cannot find the car, and she berates herself for having left Frédéric in the car and, more importantly, for having trusted him. She imagines that he will take the red skirt that Laure had found in one of her boxes and decided to keep, and give it to his wife or girlfriend. Undoubtedly the skirt will be too big and too short for her, Laure imagines. Details of Laure's appearance in the novel are scant, and they are always filtered through her awareness, her imagination. Hence the very nature of the cinema poses a dilemma of adaptation.

Crucial in this context is the way in which Laure is embodied, how she functions as a visible and concrete presence in the film. Vincent Lindon is a well-known actor in France, and he possesses a quiet, masculine presence that is somewhat evocative of Jean Gabin (hence the name "Jean" seems particularly well suited to his character). The role of Laure is played by Valérie Lemercier. Lemercier is best known as a comedian in France, and her stage shows are highly acclaimed. She has appeared in films, including *The Visitors* (Jean-Marie Poiré, 1993) in which she plays a comically awkward wealthy woman, and *Le Derrière* (1999), which she wrote and directed, and in which she plays the lead role(s), as a woman who disguises herself as a man. Lemercier has a huge gay following in France, and at the time of the release of *Le Derrière,* she appeared on the cover of *Têtu,* a French gay/lesbian magazine, as a man.

Casting Lemercier as the romantic lead in *Friday Night* was something Claire Denis was committed to from the outset, but Lemercier herself wasn't sure. "At first, I hesitated a great deal," said Lemercier. "My initial reaction, on reading the screenplay, was to feel that I didn't have my place in the story. In fact, I didn't have the nerve to accept" (Wellspring 2003: 11). Lemercier does not conform to standard notions of female beauty, especially for a film actress, and this quality makes Laure's story all the more engaging in the film. Denis has said that she always admired Lemercier, but "I also had the feeling that she never realized that she was also very attractive" (Kipp 2003: 39). More bluntly, Lemercier "felt she was too ugly to be in that film. She wanted me to choose a better looking actress. To me she is very good looking" (Hart 2003: 4).

In *Friday Night,* Lemercier is radiant in the role of Laure, and given her unconventional looks, as well as her reputation as a gay icon and a gender-bending performer, she brings to the film as much emphasis on how the character is transformed as on the sexual experience. Both are central in Bernheim's novel, but one can imagine how easily the film version (that is, if it were filmed by anyone other than Claire Denis) could turn into nothing more than a simple romance. Additionally, one can see how Denis's film might have turned into a normalization of Lemercier's boundary-crossing persona. If there is a transformation in the character of Laure in the film, it is defined in terms of her own recognition of her beauty and of her ability to live in the present tense. Of course, the sexual encounter is key, but the way it is filmed suggests much more the importance of touch and contact. Often it is difficult to know exactly which body part belongs to whom when Laure and Jean make love in the hotel room, and the scenes are shot at very close range, emphasizing sensual and sexual connection less than specific sexual acts.

From the outset, *Friday Night* is centered on Laure's consciousness, on her own transitional space as she finishes packing for the move that will take place the next day. The opening images of the film show the interior of Laure's apartment, filled with boxes. We then see shots of the rooftops of the city of Paris, and we move back to Laure's apartment as she seals some boxes. Laure moves to the window, and we see her, her back facing us, as she gazes outward. There follows a series of beautiful images of the city, where the focus is famous Parisian scenes, including the Eiffel Tower and Sacré-Coeur, as well as apartment buildings with lit windows. No people are visible until the camera shifts, and it comes as something of a shock to see that the streets below are filmed in fast motion, so that people and cars are moving at high speed. The movements across the apartment buildings and the rooftops seem slow, even languid, but the shift to the populated streets is abrupt. It is almost as if a reverie has been interrupted, as if Laure, while contemplating her place in this city, is suddenly jolted back to reality. It is not only because *Friday Night* follows *Trouble Every Day* that these scenes are suggestive of the way Paris is evoked in the earlier film. In both films, the city is regarded with wonder, and while there is a world of difference between the anxiety of moving and the anxiety of sexual violence, there is nonetheless a common denominator in the way that Paris signifies transition and liminal space.

As I have noted, the film follows the novel very closely. There are some aspects of the film that take on particular significance precisely because we see them on film, and because Denis's film work is so attentive to the ways in which glances and observations function in complex ways. Early in the novel, when Laure sees Frédéric for the first time on the street, she imagines that he is meeting a woman. "He watched the cars, all the cars. He squinted his eyes. He was looking for someone, probably a woman. They were to meet here, at this corner, so that they could go home together" (Bernheim 16). Suddenly Laure finds herself just a few yards from him: "He started walking in her direction. He found the woman waiting for him. She must be right behind her. Laure wanted to turn around to see her but she stopped herself" (Bernheim 16). The man is at the driver's window, asking Laure to give him a ride.

In the film the introduction of Jean follows these contours, but with a difference. Laure sees Jean on the street, and initially there appears to be a shot-reverse shot between the two of them (figs. 29, 30). As if to stress the importance of the exchange of looks in this scene, right before we, and Laure, see Jean, the film lingers on a large set of neon-rimmed eyeglasses, an advertisement for an optician. But very quickly, Laure becomes an observer of the woman she imagines is the person he is looking for: a conventionally beautiful blonde in a nearby car who, in a series of dissolves, smiles, tosses her hair, and applies lipstick (figs. 31, 32, 33).

This woman is one of several conventionally beautiful women who appear in the film. In the café, Laure sees Jean talking to a young woman (played by Florence Loiret-Caille, who played Christelle, the maid, in *Trouble Every Day*) and imagines that he is attracted her, and the scene is repeated in the restaurant, when a young woman (played by Hélène Fillières) again sparks Laure's insecurity. When Laure sees the woman in the car as the potential mate of Jean, the film juxtaposes a weary Laure, who rests her head on the steering wheel, and the blonde woman, who seems unaware of being observed. While it is tempting to say that Laure moves from being an observer to being a participant in the world that surrounds her, something of the observer never really leaves Lemercier's performance in the film. Indeed, this moment of juxtaposition of two women, one brunette and one blonde, one who observes and the other who is observed, is a way of addressing the question of Laure's "looks" by stressing not only, or even primarily, jealousy or rivalry, but rather the status of women who observe, who are keenly aware of the world around them.

Laure's initial encounter with Jean involves, then, a complex pattern of seeing and being seen, of observing and being aware of one's self being observed. Despite the fact that Laure has already approached a young man walking on the street (played by Grégoire Colin) who declines her offer of a ride, Jean's request for a ride still seems a bit intrusive. The city of Paris is transformed by the strike, and urban practices of anonymity break down. For a woman driving alone at night through the city streets, there is something comforting about the warmth of the car, yet something tantalizing about the possibility of an encounter that allows a connection with another being without the usual fears of violence and

Figure 29: Jean in *Friday Night*

Figure 30: Laure in *Friday Night*

Figure 31: The encounter in *Friday Night* |

Figure 32: The encounter in *Friday Night* |

Figure 33: The encounter in *Friday Night* |

danger. That may well be one of the most appealing aspects of *Friday Night*. The city of Paris that we see is not really recognizable in any but generic terms; there are no landmarks, like the Eiffel Tower or Sacré-Coeur, that we see at the beginning of the film. Laure moves through this urban space that is open to her imagination and her desires, and while there is no deadly desire like that of Coré on the prowl in *Trouble Every Day,* there is nonetheless a sense that Paris is a city of dreams and nightmares, and that in both cases a woman's desire allows us to see the city in a new way.

For the purposes of this study, *Friday Night* provides an interesting conclusion. Despite the ways it differs from other films by Denis, it also engages with two of the most prevalent aspects of her work: First, the function of memory, of film as the exploration of how the past shapes the present but can never really be contained by it, and, second, the importance of touch, of physical contact as something that is both precious and potentially frightening. Given that *Friday Night* is so resolutely a present-tense film, it may seem odd to situate it in the context of memory, but memory in Denis's work is never a straightforward matter of the present in relationship to the past. *Chocolat*'s memory work has as much to do with the memory of Ferdinand Oyono's novel, *Une Vie de boy,* as with a specific autobiographical experience. Even memories that could easily become trips down nostalgia lane, such as the memories associated with rock music of the 1960s so powerfully evoked in *U.S. Go Home,* are always situated within a framework of the complex ways that music "accompanies" excursions into the past. Nico's rendition of "These Days" at the conclusion of *U.S. Go Home* both recalls the 1960s and suggests how that era is one of painful transition as well as remembered connections.

In a more general sense, the characters in Denis's films are shaped by memories. France searches out her childhood in Cameroon, and Dah evokes a memory of Martinique when he prepares Jocelyn's body in *No Fear, No Die.* Théo wants to return to Martinique, and while we never really know exactly how much of a past he has there, the film represents Martinique in a very limited, fragmented way, in black and white photographs. Galoup's narration in *Beau travail* is a way of remembering (and understanding) the painful past in his encounter with Sentain, and the characters in *Trouble Every Day* are embodiments of "something" that happened in the past. It is tempting to describe these characters as "haunted" by memories, but that is not entirely accurate, because the films refuse to anchor memories in an easily identifiable past, or place, that can be separated from the present tense.

Rather, memories seem to "float" in Denis's films, like suspended questions. What exactly does Théo expect to find in Martinique? What happened during Nénette's and Boni's separate childhoods? Who is the father of Nénette's child? What "caused" the affliction in *Trouble Every Day?* What part of Camille's past could explain how he became a murderer? If the characters of Denis's films seem to carry certain pasts with them, the films refuse to make memories accessible, comforting, or even knowable for the spectators. Hence *Friday Night*'s present tense suggests something central to all of Denis's work. Only the effects of memory are visible, since what matters is the present tense of the films, how individuals move through memory.

Bodies meet, and characters touch in Denis's films, and *Friday Night* is an extended meditation on touch, on physical contact. There are moments of great intimacy in Denis's films, but at the same time there is a fragility, an awareness of the preciousness of touch but also of its dangers. Laure withdraws from Jean in *Friday Night* when there is the possibility that his touch might leave a mark on her skin (in the novel, this is rendered explicitly as a fear that any mark might alert François, the boyfriend, to her adventure). But when Laure leaves and walks down the street, there is a lightness, a freedom in her step. One could even call her departure a kind of dance, one of the ultimate forms of self-expression in Denis's work.

Touch tends to be fleeting, even when its results are permanent, like the hand-burning scene in *Chocolat*. The brief touch of the hands of Daïga and Camille in *I Can't Sleep* suggests the simultaneous pleasure and danger associated with physical contact. Dance has an important function in this context, since it so often signals both an exultation of the body and a displacement, a projection of something else, from Jocelyn's swaying dance with the cock in *No Fear, No Die* to Galoup's frenzied dance at the conclusion of *Beau travail*. Overall, Claire Denis's cinema in one in which bodies move through landscapes of present and past, and through the pleasure and pain of contact with others. All the while, Denis observes with the engaged curiosity of someone who loves the cinema, and who is passionate about the actors and characters with whom she develops a very special relationship.

Notes

1. Denis wrote the continuity for Rivette's unfinished film *Marie et Julien* (Rivette 2002).

2. *Chocolat* has received extensive critical attention, particularly in terms of the relationship between gender and colonialism. See, in particular, Bert Cardullo (1990), Wendy Everett (1996), Susan Hayward (2002b), E. Ann Kaplan (1997), Rosanna Maule (1999), Janice Morgan (2003), Hilary Neroni (2003), Ruth Perlmutter (1998), Catherine Portuges (1996), Michael S. Roth (1990), Diana Sandars (2001), Dina Sherzer (1996), Dana Strand (2000), and Fiona Villella (1999).

3. Three films in the series were also released as feature films under different titles. André Téchiné's film *Les Roseaux sauvages* is the expanded version (for theatrical release) of the film shown in the series. Olivier Assayas's *L'eau froide* is the feature-length version of *La Page blanche*, and Cédric Kahn's *Trop de bonheur* is the expanded version of *Le Bonheur*.

4. The filmmakers who contributed to the series *Tous les garçons et les filles de leur âge* did not consult with each other and were not necessarily aware of each other's projects. Marc-Olivier Padis has noted, nonetheless, that certain shared themes and preoccupations emerge from the series. He notes that a common motif of the nine films is a breakdown of the family as any kind of "initiator" to the world, and that the adolescents of the films find, in their own groups of

friends, an autonomy lacking in the family as well as "protection and refuge" (1996: 36, 38–39). *U.S. Go Home*'s focus on the brother-sister relationship is thus somewhat unusual in the series as a whole, for the relationship functions both as a family bond and as a social bond—bonds that tended, in the other films, to focus on parents and friends.

5. For discussions of *I Can't Sleep*, see in particular Janet Bergstrom's discussion of opacity in the film (2003) and Martine Beugnet's analyses of the film through the lens of film noir, as well as her lucid discussion of the ways in which race and racism function in the film (2000a, 2000b, 2001). For other insightful discussions of the film in terms of race and racism, see Cynthia Marker (1999) and Corinne Oster (2003). For an interesting reading of the function of pleasure in the film, see Todd McGowan (2003). For a detailed comparison of the film to the coverage of the Thierry Paulin case, see Deborah Streifford Reisinger (2000).

6. Commentary on *Beau travail* is extensive and provocative, ranging from discussions of the adaptation of Melville (Grant 2002) to masculinity (Lippe 2000), from identity (Beugnet and Sillars 2001; Bergstrom 2003) to postcoloniality (Hayward 2001).

7. Sarah Cooper's analysis of the film (2001) shows how, almost paradoxically, the juxtaposition of heterosexual desire (between the Djiboutian women at the disco and the Legionnaires in general, and between Galoup and Rahel, specifically) and the homoerotic connection (between Galoup, Forestier, and Sentain) enables a queer reading of the film.

8. For another reading of Galoup's dance, see del Rio (2003).

Interview with Claire Denis |

This interview took place in Paris in July 2003. I had spent the previous month in there, and I had the opportunity to see all of Denis's short films, which are usually not shown outside of film festivals or retrospectives. In our discussion, Denis provided background and context for many of those films. While it is unfortunate that these films are not more readily available (in France or in the United States), Denis's discussion of them gives insight into the range of her career. Denis also discussed the use of the voice-over and the influence on her work of filmmakers such as Robert Bresson, Jean-Luc Godard, and Shohei Imamura.

JUDITH MAYNE: Could you say something about your current project?

CLAIRE DENIS: It's a complex project. It's not really an adaptation; it's inspired by Jean-Luc Nancy's book *L'Intrus* [*The Intruder*, 2000]. I worked on the screenplay with Jean-Pôl Fargeau, and it's being made on a very small budget, just like *Beau travail*, and it's produced by ARTE. I made the short film *Vers Nancy* [*Towards Nancy*] for the series *Ten*

Minutes Older, because I was working on the screenplay for this full-length film. It's based on the idea of intrusion.

JM: One of the striking aspects of your career is your continuing collaboration with cinematographer Agnès Godard, screenwriter Jean-Pôl Fargeau, editor Nelly Quettier, not to mention the actors with whom you've developed a special relationship—Alex Descas, Grégoire Colin, Béatrice Dalle. This collaboration isn't just reflected in your own films; you've also appeared in the films of other directors: Laetitia Masson's *En avoir (ou pas),* Tonie Marshall's *Vénus beauté (institut).* You also have developed close relationships with other filmmakers. You share screenwriting credit, for example, with Yousry Nasrallah for his film *El Medina* [2000]. Could you talk about how that collaboration came to be?

CD: Yousry had seen *I Can't Sleep,* and he wanted me to help him work on the part of *El Medina* that takes place in Paris. We worked together in the fall of one year, and he filmed the "Paris" part of the film a year later; in between, he shot the beginning of the film that takes place in Cairo. Yousry is someone who works quickly, and who really learns from everyone he meets. He changed the "Paris" section of the film enormously from what we had worked on together. For me, what was important was not sharing the screenwriting credit, but rather it was talking to him about Paris, and sharing with him the conception of his film. When he came to Paris to shoot, I wasn't there (I was shooting on location), but by that point he had his own clear idea of the Paris sections of the film. He speaks fluent French and knows France well; I simply served as a facilitator, a fellow filmmaker, to help him create the section of the film that takes place in Paris. *El Medina* is a beautiful film, and he has just recently completed another.

JM: It has been interesting to see your short films, particularly those filmed in black and white. In some, like *Pour Ushari Ahmed Mahmoud,* the black and white seems just the right choice for the depiction of the city of Paris. Could you talk about how you came to make *Keep It for Yourself,* also a black and white film that takes place in New York? It's an intriguing film on a number of levels. Obviously, it is your only American film, and it's a very funny look at New York City as perceived by a young French woman (Sophie Simon, who also appears in *I Can't Sleep* as Mona's sister). Unfortunately, it is a difficult film to see. But it's also interesting in relationship to your later work, since this is the first time that you worked with Vincent Gallo.

CD: In a way, *Keep It for Yourself* was a bit of a joke, because it was a commissioned film. I had just made *No Fear, No Die*. Philippe Carcassonne, the producer, had begun working with Kees Kasander, in Holland. The two of them were producing Peter Greenaway's film *Pillow Book* [1996], which was in coproduction with a company in Japan. At the time, Kasander received an offer to make publicity films for Nissan, the car company, and there was a very large budget. Kasander said, why spend all of this money to make individual publicity films, when it could be used to make a feature-length film? I agreed to be a part of the film. The idea was to have a three-part film, set in three different cities, each of which used the same Nissan deluxe replica car. An Argentinian director, Alejandro Agresti, made *Library Love,* set in Paris, and Kaizo Hayashi made the film set in Tokyo, *Man from the Moon.* I was told: you'll make the film set in New York City. So I arrived in New York with the car, which was shipped over. Then I had one week to shoot the film. I met Jim Schamus, who was in charge of the production, and we really got along well. I brought a French actress (Sophie Simon) with me, and I worked with people I knew: Jim Stark, who played the next-door neighbor, had been Jim Jarmusch's producer; Sara Driver, the film director, played the part of the woman who befriends Sophie. And that is where I met Vincent Gallo for the first time.

John Lurie did the music for the film, and I was friends with him. He had worked with the Lounge Lizards, and that group split into two, and the group Jazz Passenger was formed. The man who played the "intruder" in the film, E. J. Rodriguez, was the percussionist for Jazz Passenger. All in all, *Keep It for Yourself* was really a film made with friends.

JM: One of the distinctive aspects of your career is how well you work with actors. It is obvious in your films; and in interviews, you've discussed how important it is for you to create and maintain a special bond with actors. You've used terms like "solidarity" to describe your relationships with actors. I've been able to see televised interviews with you and actors from your films, and it is really quite amazing to see you "in person," as it were, with these artists. Your special and unique relationship with them is obvious. Alice Houri [*U.S. Go Home* and *Nénette and Boni*] and

Béatrice Dalle [*I Can't Sleep* and *Trouble Every Day*] are two very different actresses, at different stages of their careers when they worked with you: Houri was a young teenager, and she seems quite shy in the public eye, whereas Dalle is a well-known actress with a very strong, sometimes very intense, public persona. I mention these two because I happened to see interviews where you appeared with them, one right after the other, and the relationship you developed with these two very different people was so extraordinarily visible. Even through all of the conventions of the televised interview, you can really feel how much you connect with your actors, and how much they connect with you (in an interview about *Nénette and Boni,* another participant in the show, who had nothing to do with the film, even commented on what a wonderful relationship you had with Houri, just on the basis of the televised program alone!). You can sense the affinity; it is almost magical.

CD: Alice Houri was fourteen when I met her (she lied about her age to get the part in *U.S. Go Home*). She is an extraordinary girl. It's true, I have a vital connection with her, and it's not a maternal connection. I've maintained a very strong connection with her.

JM: Obviously collaboration is a central part of your career. Yet it is rare for you to adapt a text written by someone else; even the adaptation of Emmanuèle Bernheim's novel *Vendredi soir,* which you've described as a very "close," i.e., literal, rendering of the novel, was cowritten by you and the novelist. I'm curious about how your collaborative work with actors extends to situations like the one with Jacques Nolot [who appeared in *Nénette and Boni* and *J'ai pas sommeil*], when you are not only working with the actor as an actor, but as a writer as well, as is the case in *The Hoop Skirt.*

CD: I made *The Hoop Skirt* for ARTE. Playwrights were asked to write a monologue, and then several filmmakers were asked to film the monologues. Jacques wrote his, a monologue in a woman's voice. I said to him—this is crazy, you are the one who wrote the text, it is so close to you, you are the only person who can really recite this monologue. So we came up with the idea that he would recite the monologue to a woman who listens. I know Jacques very well, and he thought that I understood his text quite well.

In *I Can't Sleep,* Nolot's role was supposed to have been much bigger. [*When Daïga runs into a movie theater to escape a man who is pursuing her on the street, she sits next to Jacques Nolot. The scene is hilarious; Daïga didn't realize she was in a porn theater. She is surrounded by men who look at her as if she were an alien creature. She bursts out laughing. —JM*][1] The scene in which he appears, in the porn theater, was partially responsible for the film which he wrote and directed that takes place entirely in a porn theater, *La chatte à deux têtes* [*Porn Theater*] which came out last year [2002].

In *I Can't Sleep,* the scene with Nolot was initially longer, and he invites Daïga to dinner. The scene was quite long. The film was completed just before the Cannes festival, and there was a moment of panic. The producer said the film is too long; you have to shorten it. I think he (the producer) really wanted me to cut that particular scene. I said okay, I cut the scene, I said, it's probably a good idea. . . . and later I really regretted it. That was the only time I had to cut a scene.

JM: Of all of the films I've had an opportunity to see—i.e., the short films, like those we've just discussed, and films that aren't easily available—the one that I think of as a great revelation is *U.S. Go Home.* Unfortunately it isn't distributed in the U.S.

CD: It has been shown in the U.S., but no, it isn't distributed there. ARTE—the producers of the televised series *All the Boys and Girls of Their Age,* for which *U.S. Go Home* was made—had a small budget, but great musical freedom. For the televised series, the films could only be sixty minutes long, which is too short for a commercial release, and the cost of paying musical rights for a commercial release would be enormous.

JM: Why is it that some films in the series—like those of André Téchiné and Olivier Assayas—are feature-length films?[2]

CD: Those directors said, we'll do the television series, but we're going to make feature-length films, and then you can show shorter versions for ARTE. I was the last one who signed on for the series, because I was shooting *I Can't Sleep. U.S. Go Home* had to be completed in September, and I began shooting in July. Every time someone wanted to make a feature-length film (to be shortened for the television screening), it was in conflict with the contract and involved a big debate with ARTE. I said, fine, I have two months to complete the film, and I don't want to get into this complication. Téchiné completed shooting very early, and there was a long discussion about whether he could do the feature-length film, and Olivier Assayas also finished a good year before I did. There I was, in the space of two months I had to shoot, edit, and complete the film to have it to ARTE by September. I said, fine, I won't pursue the option of a feature-length film.

JM: How did you come to direct *Nice, Very Nice,* which stars one of your favorite actors, Grégoire Colin?[3]

CD: That was a strange thing. The guy who proposed the film wanted us to do an homage to Jean Vigo's film *A Propos de Nice* [1930]. I was in the midst of preparing *Nénette and Boni.* I said, listen, what you are asking would require a year's worth of work to do it well, to do a real work of commentary on Vigo's film. I preferred to use this as an opportunity to do some preparation for *Nénette and Boni.* I had read in the newspaper about a young man, in Nice, who was ordered to kill another man who was a pizza-maker, and that became the subject of my film.

JM: One of the most intriguing films you've made is also quite unlike anything else you've done: *A propos d'une déclaration* [*About a Declaration*]. Many of your films are about sexuality, but this one—in which a woman shaves her pubic hair in a bathtub while a rubber duck looks on—is nonetheless quite distinct.

CD: When I was commissioned to do the film, it wasn't to be projected on a screen; it was to be part of an installation at the Cartier Foundation. The exhibition included paintings and sculptures, and four filmmakers were invited to make video installations that would be looped, continuously on display. The other filmmakers were Olivier Assayas, Raymond Depardon, and André Bonzel [*eventually Hal Hartley and Nacer Khemir were included as well—JM*]. When I was invited to participate in the project, Philippe Sollers was the curator, and the exhibition was called "The Declaration of Love" (eventually it was called "Love"). So I began with my portable digital camera, and since the theme of the exhibition was "a declaration of love," I thought of Nagisa Oshima, and of how, in *In the Realm of Passion,* the man asks the woman to shave her pubic area for him. Sollers and I had talked about Oshima, and the film I made was an homage to that scene. Afterwards, the Cartier Foundation thought that the film was too "indecent" for their exhibition, and they asked me to make a film about "Love" in general, and therefore to get rid of what they found offensive. Sollers insisted that my film remain as a part of the exhibit. What interested me was a film about that scene in *In the Realm of Passion,* but I was doing publicity for another film at the time, and I was working on *A propos d'une déclaration* in the evenings. By the time I was finished with the film, Cartier removed things from the original exhibition. Once they removed the scene from Oshima's film, the exhibit was much more general, about "love" rather than specifically about the declaration of love. They no longer wanted my film; they thought it was offensive; Sollers was the one who insisted that my film remain.

JM: Could you talk about the film you directed for Amnesty International, *Pour Ushari Ahmed Mahmoud?* It's quite beautiful.

CD: When Amnesty International invited me to make a film, there were twenty cases that were to be featured in the films. Amnesty International's approach is to select a particular case and to write letters to the president on behalf of the individual. For the series of films, Amnesty International had an idea that I thought was a good one: each film would be a joint effort with two people, i.e., a writer would work with an actress, a director with an actor, etc. The principle of each film was the reading of a letter. I said, listen, I really don't know how to choose "my prisoner," I will make the film about whichever prisoner you like. So they proposed a Sudanese man, a professor, who was in prison. Alain Souchon, my partner for the film, who is a singer, and I made the film. We began by writing a letter that Alain would read aloud in the film. Then I said, listen, Alain, since you're a singer it might be better for you to "sing" the letter. But when we were ready, Amnesty International learned that the prisoner might be released. So they told us, don't say his name aloud in the film, because if you do, they might take it the wrong way and send him back to prison.

I went to twenty different rooming houses in Belleville, and I found two young Sudanese men who barely spoke French, and I asked them to participate in the film. They did.

JM: On various web sites, I've seen reference to other films by you, but they don't seem to be distributed. For example, *Portrait of Jean-Louis Murat* [*a popular singer in France who wrote the title song for* I Can't Sleep, *as well as the song—* "Le lien défait" *—that Camille lip-syncs in his performance—JM*].

CD: That film was never completed. I worked with Yousry Nasrallah on it, in Egypt. We all enjoyed making the film, but the record producer didn't think it was good publicity for Jean-Louis Murat. They refused to pay for the completion of the film, which angered me a bit, but I said, sooner or later, I'll finish the film myself. I've tried to recover the rights for the film, so that Jean-Louis and I can finish it ourselves.

JM: . . . and *Boom-Boom?*

CD: That was the original title for *U.S. Go Home.* "Boom" is the French word for party, and there is a Chuck Berry song called "Boom Boom." I didn't use the song in the film, so I changed the title.

JM: . . . .and *Ni une ni deux* [*Neither One Nor Two*]?

CD: *Ni une ni deux* is a film I began to make for Antenne 2 [*a French television company—JM*], about Cameroonian women—one was a television announcer, one was a pharmacist, another was a city planner, and another was a deputy. They all had fairly important jobs. They spoke about how difficult and impossible their lives were, even though Cameroon is not—compared to other countries—a horrible place. But for them, life was really hard—doing their jobs, raising their children, living with their husbands. They were always in conflict with their in-laws, who thought that their careers were too important in their lives. That was the theme. These were brilliant women. The film was never finished because, first of all, the producer was having enormous production problems at the time, and, second, Antenne 2 wanted me to do a voice-over. All of the women spoke French with a slight Cameroonian accent, but Antenne 2 wanted a voice-over. I said I thought it was a shame that these women couldn't speak for themselves, that it had to be me who told their stories. So that became a matter of principle for me. There was no reason why they couldn't speak for themselves. I said, listen, this just isn't right. Why does there always have to be this exoticizing means of separating the voice from the person? The women spoke very well. So that was that . . .

JM: You've spoken, in interviews, about voice-overs, and how they never work unless they are really an integral part of the film.

CD: This was different, because this was using the voice-over to objectify the women, so it wasn't acceptable to me. There are many films with voice-overs that I like, but I think it's very difficult to do well. The voice-over has to be very clearly defined; either it is the voice of the filmmaker or the voice of a character in the film. For me, the most beautiful example of voice-over is Godard's *Le Petit soldat.* Michel Subor [as Bruno Forestier] does the voice-over, but it is Godard who is speaking. For me, that is a perfect example of a voice-over. I don't think I've ever really succeeded with a voice-over. The voice-over is a strong expression of the filmmaker's position in regards to the film. In other words, does the director need to be in the film? For me, it's as if I'm already in the film, in other ways. To me, doing a voice-over is like redoing the same film, adding something once it is completed, and that's not something I've been able to do. Maybe someday I'll find myself in a situation where I want to do a voice-over, but it hasn't happened yet.

I made the effort for *Beau travail,* because that film is somewhat dedicated to *Le Petit soldat.* Denis Lavant's [as Galoup] first spoken words are the last sentence of *Le Petit soldat.*

JM: But in *No Fear, No Die,* Dah has a voice-over, particularly in the beginning of the film.

CD: Sort of, yes, because we were quoting Chester Himes.

JM: There is an interesting play with the voice-over in that film. At the very beginning of the film, we see the Chester Himes quotation as a title, and then Dah repeats the quotation in voice-over. Then he says, "I don't know who said that, but it isn't important." The scene reminded me of the beginning to another Godard film, *Two or Three Things I Know about Her* [1967], when Godard recites an introduction to the actress Marina Vlady, and he says almost exactly the same thing: "Now, she's turning her head to the left, but it isn't important" [Godard 1971: 21].

CD: Perhaps . . . I thought it was in Dah's character not to know who the quotation was from. You come to the cinema with your experiences and your life, and Godard came to the cinema as someone who had written about the cinema, so perhaps he felt the need to continue to write about his work in the form of the voice-over. As for me, I lived in a world where Godard's extraordinary and revitalizing creative force was difficult to take on as any kind of model. Instead, his films were to be loved and admired, as I love *Le Petit soldat.* But in my admiration, I don't want to reproduce something, to imitate it, because I would feel ridiculous doing so . . .

JM: But there are very strong ways in which your films admire other films and other filmmakers without ever being imitations or copies. I suspect that you really love the films of Robert Bresson. Take the scene in *I Can't Sleep,* where the first murder of an old woman is presented (well over halfway into the film). The woman opens the outside door to the apartment complex, and she is followed by Camille and Raphael. It is very quiet, except for the footsteps of the old woman, clicking across the pavement. You've described that scene as borrowing a bit from the codes of the horror film, using silence and the sounds of footsteps to suggest suspense and anxiety and the sense that something bad is about to happen. But for me that scene is a strong evocation of Bresson, and the ways in which the exaggerated sounds of footsteps mark the passage of human movement, as well as the sense of space that is filled, but also hollowed out, by the presence of human beings. In the scene in *I Can't Sleep,* the footsteps become, briefly, the center of the scene, and they mark the presence as well as the absence of the old woman.

There are many moments in your films that evoke Bresson, from the footsteps in *I Can't Sleep,* to the vast, seemingly "empty" spaces of Djibouti that are inhabited by the Legionnaires in *Beau travail.* In saying this, I don't mean to suggest that your work is in any way derivative, or even that your films are homages to Bresson (or any other director). Rather, it is as if there is a consciousness, in your films, of cinematic traditions, of cinematic history, and of cinematic authorship. In your films, you reflect upon what cinema is, and that reflection seems to take you across different traditions and different moments in the conception of the cinema.

CD: It's true; it's difficult to have seen even just one film by Bresson and not to have been marked by the experience. The first Bresson film I ever saw (I was quite young) was *Mouchette* [1967]. I had the impression that this was a very concrete and brutal way to approach cinema. I think often of this film, because I had the impression that, above and beyond Georges Bernanos [*whose novella was the basis for the film—JM*], or religion, or purity, or a pure soul and its contamination, there was something very concrete. Later I might have intellectualized this concreteness, because now I can think of *Mouchette* in different terms. I was a teenager when I saw the film. It felt like a film of the time. When I saw Bresson's film *The Devil, Probably* [1977], I felt it was a film about my life, about people my age in a Paris that I knew—perhaps a little more bourgeois than I was, but I felt as though the film was grounded in the concrete, in my own life.

One never forgets Bresson. Admiration is a very complicated thing. It's like an alchemy; you admire something and then one day you realize that this admiration has permeated your skin. You don't have to say: "Am I going to approach this situation as Bresson might have? Or not?" It's there, it's a reflex. Then afterwards you might say to yourself—aha, yes, perhaps that was a Bressonian moment.

JM: The moment in *I Can't Sleep* when Daïga follows Camille to a café and there is that brief fluttering touch of their hands—that seems to me a very Bressonian moment.

CD: That light touch, yes . . . the scene was written to be very brief; they met in the café; he looked at her; she looked at him, and she wanted him to know that she knew, that she understood. We had very little time to shoot that scene, and the mise-en-scène was done very quickly and very simply. And it was only afterwards that I said to myself, yes, that works. But at the time, there was the street, the café, and little by little we moved towards that one moment when they touch.

JM: It's a beautiful moment in the film. The reception of *I Can't Sleep* was complex; many saw you as reviving the Thierry Paulin case, even though the film doesn't work in any way as a "serial killer" film. I love your films, yet I was fearful of seeing *I Can't Sleep*! Like many people, I wondered how you could possibly succeed in making a film about a black, gay, HIV-positive serial killer, without falling into the very stereotypes that characterized news reports about Paulin in the first place. But you made an amazing film that takes the recognition of murder and violence to a whole other level. Now I know you've said that you don't like provocation, but how is it that you are drawn to these potentially controversial subjects?

CD: I don't like provocation because I take no pleasure in provoking people. You have to enjoy provocation to do it, and I don't. I always approach situations with curiosity, and sometimes my curiosity might make me audacious. But the motivation for my curiosity is never the desire to provoke. One day someone proposed that I adapt a true crime [*fait divers*] story—not the Paulin case. I worked on that project, and after six months, I realized that it didn't really interest me, so I dropped it. The people who had proposed the topic, including the producer Philippe Carcassonne, said, well, what true crime story does interest you? And I said that I'd like to work on an obscure true crime story, one that hasn't received so much attention and commentary, one that would retain an aura of mystery for me. What had always interested me in the Paulin case was that people who knew him thought he was a very nice guy . . . and also the fact that, one day, a mother reads the newspaper and sees her son described as a monster. That is something very strange, very odd. With true crime stories, journalists know that it's good to get an interview with the mother, or the brother, or the sister of the criminal. It brings an emotional hook to the story. But this is also the most uncomfortable thing, because one has to say to the mother: Your son is a monster. He was the monster of the eighteenth arrondissement, and even his lawyers were relieved when he died before the trial began. In France, there isn't a popular media conception of the "serial killer" like there is in the U.S. People were baffled by Paulin, and by the fact that the murders were not sexual.

When I agreed to use the Paulin case as the inspiration for the film, I said that I would focus on the people who knew him. I wouldn't focus on him. So I made a film about the people who knew him without knowing what he did. That, I thought, I can do. Jean-Pôl Fargeau and I worked for two years without stopping, but then we did stop because I began to have terrible doubts about what I was doing. And I asked myself, who is going to be willing to produce a film like this? Finally Olivier Assayas introduced me to Bruno Pesery. I told Olivier that I wasn't afraid myself, but I was afraid of not being able to communicate with a producer about a project like this. Pesery was willing to embark on the adventure, and so it happened. But frankly there was always the feeling of being a bit in the dark, and I tried to translate that in the film. There was a circular movement around him, and then he died. He evaporated.

JM: When you think about the work of an individual filmmaker, like I'm obviously doing in the book I'm writing on your films, it's hard not to think about which film is your favorite. But perhaps a more interesting way to think about "favorites" is to ask what film, or films, made a difference. I don't remember exactly when I saw *Chocolat* for the first time, but I believe it was shortly after it was released in 1988. The film was widely acclaimed, and people I knew were discussing the film in relationship to postcoloniality, to autobiography, to the relationship between past and present. But what has always stayed with me, in *Chocolat,* is that incredible ending: the adult France, with a slight smile on her face, turns away from the window at the airport. We then see the three Cameroonian men loading the plane and then taking a break. The camera approaches them and then stops. The scene lasts a fairly long time, and it's a beautiful conclusion, one that rests on a kind of ambiguity—the woman whose memories have taken us to the colonial past has moved out of frame, and we are seeing—at a reserved distance—a moment of friendship between men. France's return has been neither happy nor tragic, but the film takes us away from her and towards something else.

When I saw *I Can't Sleep,* I thought that this entire film followed, in a way, from the conclusion of *Chocolat.* Seeing *I Can't Sleep* for the first time, I felt as though I was seeing something I had never seen before on screen. It felt like love at first sight.

CD: For me too, because that film was a real process of discovery. I understood the film while I was making it, because while making it, I was sharing the film with the actors. In that particular film, the actors became real partners. They weren't people who just showed up in the morning; they were really involved in the film. The young man who played the role inspired by Thierry Paulin [Richard Courcet], he wasn't an actor; he was completely invested in the project of the film. Jean-Pôl and I worked on the screenplay, but when it was embodied by the actors . . . Béatrice Dalle said it better than I could: "What was written on paper became flesh." All of a sudden, the violence on paper became something very different. The day that we began to film, there was desire, as if all of the different elements of the film had come into place.

There is a film by Shohei Imamura, called *Intentions of Murder,* which was made in the sixties. I saw it in the 1980s; Serge Daney had talked about it, and one summer in Paris there was a retrospective of Imamura's films. When Imamura spoke of the film, he said that it was the story of a sow. The film tells the story of a young Japanese woman, on the heavy side, who is forced into marriage to a man who doesn't love her. She is totally and completely a prisoner of this marriage. One day, her husband is away on business, and she is alone in the house. A thief breaks into the house and initially he doesn't see her. He is stealing things, and then she moves, and he sees her. He rapes her. At that moment, her life turns upside down. She has been so abandoned, and so mistreated, that she says hardly anything; for her, her body is useless flesh, and her role in life, as an object purchased by her husband, is to be the "female." All of a sudden, the rape makes her aware that this violent act is preferable to the relationship she has with her husband; she feels she has more dignity as a woman who is raped than as a woman married to her husband. The man who raped her looked at her, whereas for her husband she was nothing but an inert object. The woman begins to go out in the afternoon, when her husband is at work, and she begins to have an independent life. Then, one day, the rapist comes back. They see each other, and she leaves behind everything—her husband, her child, everything—to be with him.

This film was also based on a true story. I found the film to be extraordinary, because a violent action reveals something very unexpected—the awareness that one is alive, even though the violent action is truly horrible. Things that you just assume about life can suddenly take shape in an event—it doesn't necessarily have to be a violent event—and all of a sudden, you realize that you exist, there, in that event.

JM: Much has been made of the fact that your films demonstrate a real curiosity about men. You collaborate with both men [Fargeau] and women [Agnès Godard, Nelly Quettier], and despite the common assumption that your films are male-centered, there are great female characters in your films as well—Nénette in *Nénette and Boni,* Coré in *Trouble Every Day,* Laure in *Friday Night.* How do you see yourself as a "woman filmmaker"?

CD: I never think about the question. I think about it when a film is completed, but rarely do I think about it beforehand. Since I'm a woman, I always have the impression that the film is "female" from the outset, but I share it with men and with women. So the film becomes a relationship—with Jean-Pôl Fargeau, with Agnès Godard—and that is what's important, the relationship. Even if I'm at the origin of the film, and the film is therefore "feminine," the work of filmmaking is a relationship. It's a relationship with the actors, and it is a very erotic relationship. One day Béatrice Dalle said to me, "I'm heterosexual, and if Claire were a man we'd be married by now!" And I understand what she was saying, because when you make a film, when you share the making of a film, it's very intense.

You can't do something that isn't part of who you are. When male directors move towards female characters—something they've done quite a bit of—that's where their desire, whether it's heterosexual or homosexual, crystallizes, around the representation of a female icon. It's all about desire. . . .

Notes

1. In the original screenplay for *I Can't Sleep,* Nolot's character speaks at length to Daïga's character in the porn cinema, and they leave together to have dinner. For a complete description and dialogue of the scene, see the original screenplay (Denis and Fargeau 1997: 65–66).

2. Three films in the series were also released as feature films under different titles. André Téchiné's film *Les Roseaux sauvages* is the expanded version (for theatrical release) of the film shown in the series. Olivier Assayas's *L'eau froide* is the feature-length version of *La Page blanche,* and Cédric Kahn's *Trop de bonheur* is the expanded version of *Le Bonheur.*

3. The film is a short (ten minutes) contribution to the omnibus film *A Propos de Nice, la suite,* in which nine different filmmakers participated.

Feature Films

Chocolat (1988)
France, West Germany
Production: Cinemanuel, Marin Karmitz-MK2 Productions, Cerito Films, Wim
  Wenders Produktion, La S.E.P.T., Caroline Productions, le F.O.D.I.C., TF1
  Films Production, W.D.R. Cologne
Producers: Alain Belmondo, Gerard Crosnier, Marin Karmitz
Distribution: MK2
Direction: Claire Denis
Screenplay: Claire Denis, Jean-Pôl Fargeau
Cinematography: Robert Alazraki
Assistant Camera: Agnès Godard
Editing: Claudine Merlin
Music: Abdullah Ibrahim
Cast: Isaach de Bankolé (Protée), Guilia Boschi (Aimée Dalens), François Cluzet
  (Marc Dalens), Jean-Claude Adelin (Luc), Laurent Arnal (Machinard), Jean
  Bediebe (Prosper), Jean-Quentin Châtelain (Courbassol), Emmanuelle Chau-
  let (Mireille Machinard), Kenneth Cranham (Jonathan Boothby), Jacques
  Denis (Joseph Delpich), Cécile Ducasse (France as a girl), Clementine Es-
  sono (Marie-Jeanne), Didier Flamand (Captain Védrine), Essindi Mindja
  (Blaise), Mireille Perrier (France Dalens), Emmet Judson Williamson (Mungo
  Park)
Color
105 minutes

S'en Fout la mort (*No Fear, No Die*; 1990)
France
Production: Cinéa, Pyramide, Les Films du Mindif, La Sept Cinéma, NEF Film
  Produktion, Camera One
Producer: Francis Boespflug, Philippe Carcassonne
Distribution: Pyramide

Direction: Claire Denis
Screenplay: Claire Denis, Jean-Pôl Fargeau
Cinematography: Pascal Marti
Camera Operator: Agnès Godard
Editing: Dominique Auvray
Music: Abdullah Ibrahim
Cast: Isaach de Bankolé (Dah), Alex Descas (Jocelyn), Solveig Dommartin (Toni), Christopher Buchholz (Michel), Jean-Claude Brialy (Pierre Ardennes), Christa Lang (Toni's mother), Gilbert Felmar (Ti Emile), Daniel Bellus (Henri), François Oloa Biloa (François)
Color
91 minutes

J'ai pas sommeil (*I Can't Sleep*; 1994)
France
Production: France 3 Cinéma, Canal +, Véga Film, M6 Films, Les Films du Mindif, Pyramide, Orsans Productions, Arena Films, Agora Film
Producer: Bruno Pesery and Fabienne Vonier
Distribution: Pyramide
Direction: Claire Denis
Screenplay: Claire Denis, Jean-Pôl Fargeau
Cinematography: Agnès Godard
Editing: Nelly Quettier
Music: Jean-Louis Murat, John Pattison
Cast: Katerina Golubeva (Daïga), Richard Courcet (Camille), Vincent Dupont (Raphael), Laurent Grevill (the doctor), Alex Descas (Théo), Irina Grjebina (Mina), Tolsty (Ossip), Line Renaud (Ninon), Béatrice Dalle (Mona), Sophie Simon (Alice), Simone Bonte (Ninon's mother), Antoine Chappey (car buyer), Dani (dressmaker), Solveig Dommartin (blonde woman), Catherine Frot (the woman in the apartment), Manuela Gourary (Mona's mother), Arlette Havet (victim), Alice Hurtaux (victim), Fabienne Mai (victim), Ira Mandella-Paul (Harry), Jacques Nolot (the audience member in the pornography theater)
Color
110 minutes

U.S. Go Home (1994)
France
Production: IMA Productions, La Sept-Arte
Producer: Georges Benayoun
Distribution: Dacia Films
Direction: Claire Denis
Screenplay: Claire Denis, Anne Wiazemsky
Cinematography: Agnès Godard

Editing: Dominique Auvray

Music: "Good Morning Little School Girl" (The Yardbirds); "Le Chef de la Bande" (Franck Alamo); "Hey Gyp" (Eric Burdon and the Animals); "I Believe to My Soul" (The Animals); "Adieu a un Ami" [Tribute to Buddy Holly] (Ronnie Bird); "SLC Jerk" (Les Lionceaux); "Wooly Bully" (Sam the Sham and the Pharaohs); "How You've Changed" (The Animals); "House of the Rising Sun" (The Animals); "With a Girl Like You" (The Troggs); "Try a Little Tenderness" (Otis Redding); "My Lover's Prayer" (Otis Redding); "Wild Thing" (The Troggs); "The Girl Can't Help It" (The Animals); "We've Gotta Get Out of This Place" (The Animals); "In the Midnight Hour" (The Young Rascals); "Bring It on Home to Me" (The Animals); "Ma vie s'enfuit" (Ronnie Bird); "Al Capone" (Prince Buster); "These Days" (Nico)

Cast: Alice Houri (Martine), Jessica Tharaud (Marlène), Grégoire Colin (Alain), Martine Gautier (mother), Vincent Gallo (Captain Brown)

Color

64 minutes

Nénette et Boni (*Nénette and Boni*; 1996)

France

Production: Dacia Films, La Sept Cinéma

Producer: Georges Benayoun

Distribution: Pyramide

Direction: Claire Denis

Screenplay: Claire Denis, Jean-Pôl Fargeau

Cinematography: Agnès Godard

Editing: Yann Dedet

Music: Tindersticks

Cast: Grégoire Colin (Boni), Alice Houri (Nénette), Jacques Nolot (Monsieur Luminaire), Valéria Bruni-Tedeschi (the proprietress of the bakery, "*la boulangère*"), Vincent Gallo (Vincenzo Brown), Malek Sultan (Malek), Gerard Meylan (a friend of Boni), Sebastien Pons (a friend of Boni), Mounir Aissa, Christophe Carmona (a friend of Boni), Djellali El'Ouzeri (a friend of Boni), Alex Descas (the gynecologist), Jamila Farah (the midwife), Agnes Regolo (the lab technician), Pepette (the social worker), Guy Leonardi (the counterfeit card seller), Richard Courcet (man in the station), Christine Var (the Vietnamese woman on the telephone)

Color

103 minutes

Beau travail (*Good Work*; 1999–2000)

France

Production: SM Films, La Sept-Arte, Tanais Com

Producers: Patrick Grandperret, Jérôme Minet

Distribution: Pyramide
Direction: Claire Denis
Screenplay: Claire Denis, Jean-Pôl Fargeau, inspired by the story *Billy Budd, Sailor* by Herman Melville
Cinematography: Agnès Godard
Editing: Nelly Quettier
Music: Eran Teur
Choreography: Bernardo Montet
Cast: Denis Lavant (Galoup), Michel Subor (Commander Bruno Forestier), Grégoire Colin (Gilles Sentain), Richard Courcet (Legionnaire), Nicolas Duvauchelle (Legionnaire), Adiatou Massudi (Legionnaire), Mickael Ravovski (Legionnaire), Dan Herzberg (Legionnaire), Giuseppe Molino (Legionnaire), Gianfranco Poddighe (Legionnaire), Marc Veh (Legionnaire), Thong Duy Nguyen (Legionnaire), Jean-Yves Vivet (Legionnaire), Bernardo Montet (Legionnaire), Dimitri Tsiapkinis (Legionnaire), Djamel Zemali (Legionnaire), Abdelkader Bouti (Legionnaire), Marta Tafesse Kassa (Rahel)
Color
90 minutes

Trouble Every Day (2001)
France
Production: Rezo Productions, Messaoud/a Films, Arte France Cinéma, Dacia Films, Kinétique Inc.
Producers: Georges Benayoun, Philippe Liégeois, Jean-Michel Rey
Distribution: Rezo Productions
Direction: Claire Denis
Screenplay: Claire Denis, Jean-Pôl Fargeau
Cinematography: Agnès Godard
Editing: Nelly Quettier
Music: Tindersticks
Cast: Vincent Gallo (Shane), Tricia Vessey (June), Béatrice Dalle (Coré), Alex Descas (Léo), Florence Loiret-Caille (Christelle), Hélène Lapiower (Malecot), Aurore Clément (Jeanne), Bakary Sangare (night guard), Lionel Goldstein (receptionist), Arnaud Churin (truck driver), Slimane Brahimi (friend of Christelle's), Alice Houri (young girl on train), Nelli Zargarian (chambermaid 1), Rosa Nikolic (chambermaid 2), Csilla Lukacs-Molnar (chambermaid 3), Lacrita Massix (flight attendant), Myriam Theodoresco (one of the lovers), Alexandre Uzureau de Martynoff (one of the lovers)
Color
101 minutes

Vendredi soir (*Friday Night*; 2002)
France
Production: Arena Films, France 2 Cinéma
Producer: Bruno Pesery
Distribution: BAC Distribution
Direction: Claire Denis
Screenplay: Claire Denis and Emmanuèle Bernheim, based on the novel *Vendredi soir* by Emmanuèle Bernheim
Cinematography: Agnès Godard
Editing: Nelly Quettier
Music: Dickon Hinchcliffe
Cast: Valérie Lemercier (Laure), Vincent Lindon (Jean), Hélène de Saint-Pere (Marie), Hélène Fillières (the tired woman in the restaurant), Florence Loiret-Caille (the young woman in the café), Grégoire Colin (the young man in a parka), Gilles D'Ambra (the husband in the restaurant), Micha Lescot (the hotel receptionist)
Color
90 minutes

Documentaries and Short Films

Man No Run (1989)
France
Production: Casa Films
Producer: Michel Siksik
Distribution: Documentaire sur Grand Ecran
Direction: Claire Denis
Cinematography: Pascal Marti
Editing: Dominique Auvray
Music: Les Têtes Brûlées
Cast: Les Têtes Brûlées
Color
90 minutes

Cinéma de notre temps: Jacques Rivette, le veilleur (*Cinema of Our Time: Jacques Rivette, Watchman*; 1990)
France
Production: La Sept Cinéma, AMIP, Art Productions, Channel Four Films
Direction: Claire Denis
Cinematography: Agnès Godard, Beatrice Mizrahi
Editing: Dominique Auvray, Jean Dubreuil
Music: Jean-Pierre Laforce, Henri Maikoff

Cast: Serge Daney, Claire Denis, Bulle Ogier, Jacques Rivette, Jean-François
 Stevenin
Color
124 minutes

Keep It for Yourself (1991)
U.S.
Production: Good Machine
Producer: James Schamus
Direction: Claire Denis
Screenplay: Claire Denis
Cinematography: Agnès Godard
Editing: Dominique Auvray
Music: John Lurie
Cast: Sophie Simon, Sarina Chan, Michael James, E. J. Rodriguez, Jim Stark,
 James Schamus, Michael Stun, Vincent Gallo, Sara Driver
Black and white
40 minutes

Pour Ushari Ahmed Mahmoud, segment in *Contre l'oubli* (*Against Oblivion;*
 1991)
France
Producer: Amnesty International
Distribution: Films du Paradoxe
Direction: Claire Denis
Screenplay: Claire Denis, Alain Souchon
Cinematography: Agnès Godard
Editing: Dominque Auvray
Music: Alain Souchon
Cast: Alain Souchon, Haroun Tazieff, Gerald Thomassin
Black and white
4 minutes

La Robe à Cerceau (*The Hoop Skirt;* 1992)
France
Producers: Les Poissons Volants, La Sept-Arte
Screenplay: Jacques Nolot, Claire Denis
Cinematography: Agnès Godard
Cast: Jacques Nolot, Dani
Black and white
24 minutes

Duo (1995)
Production: KONINCK for the Arts Council of England and BBC Television
Producers: Keith Griffiths, Diane Freeman
Direction: Claire Denis
Featuring *Duo,* by artist Jacques Loustal
Cast: Alex Descas
Color
4 minutes

Nice, Very Nice (segment in *A propos de Nice, la suite;* 1995)
France
Production: François Margolin
Direction: Claire Denis
Cast: Grégoire Colin, Thierry Said Bouibil, Jerome Chabreyrie, Andres Perez,
    Alain Saint-Alix, Jerome Validire
Color
10 minutes

A propos d'une déclaration (*About a Declaration*; 1997)
France
Direction: Claire Denis
Cast: Alex Descas
Color
2 minutes

Vers Nancy (Towards Nancy) in *Ten Minutes Older: The Cello* (2002)
UK, Germany
Production: Why Not Productions
Producers: Ulrich Felsberg, Nicolas McClintock, Nigel Thomas
Direction: Claire Denis
Screenplay: Claire Denis
Cinematography: Agnès Godard
Editing: Emmanuelle Pencalet
Music: Brice LeBoucq
Cast: Alex Descas, Jean-Luc Nancy, Ana Samardzija
Black and white
10 minutes

Adler, Laure, interviewer. *Cinéma*. Television series. Cercle de Minuit, La France 2. January 28, 1997.

Affergan, Francis. "Zooanthropology of the Cockfight in Martinique." *The Cockfight: A Casebook*. Ed. Alan Dundes. Madison: University of Wisconsin Press, 1986; rpt. 1994, trans. Antonella Bertoli Johnston and Alan Dundes. 191–207.

Alberge, Dalya. "Director Defends Cannes Film's Brutal Sex Scenes." *Times of London*, May 8, 2001. 10/12/01 <http://www.thetimes.co.uk/article/0,2-125794,00.html>.

Ancian, Aimé. "Claire Denis: An Interview." *Senses of Cinema* 23 (November–December 2002). 15/08/03 <http://www.sensesofcinema.com/contents/02/23/denis interview.html>.

Ang, Ien. "Hegemony-in-Trouble: Nostalgia and the Ideology of the Impossible in European Cinema." *Screening Europe: Image and Identity in Contemporary European Cinema*. Ed. Duncan Petrie. London: British Film Institute, 1992. 21–31.

Assayas, Olivier, et al. "Quelques vagues plus tard." *Cahiers du Cinéma* hors-série (1998): 70–75.

Audé, Françoise, and Yann Tobin. "Entretien avec Agnès Godard." *Positif* 471 (May 2000): 131–36.

Azoury, Philippe. "En Écho aux photos de Jeff Wall." *Libération* [Paris], July 11, 2001: 6.

Benjamin, Sonia. "Claire Denis, une cinéaste curieuse de toutes les cultures." *Journal Français d'Amérique*, August 4–31, 1995: 10.

Bergstrom, Janet. "Opacity in the Films of Claire Denis." *French Civilization and Its Discontents: Nationalism, Colonialism, Race*. Ed. Tyler Stovall and Georges Van Den Abbeele. Lanham, Md.: Lexington Books, 2003. 69–101.

Bernheim, Emmanuèle. *Vendredi soir*. Paris: Gallimard; Folio, 1998; rpt. 2000.

Beugnet, Martine. "Film Noir, Mort Blanche: *J'ai Pas Sommeil*, Claire Denis (1995)." *(Ab)Normalities*. Ed. Catherine Dousteyssier-Khoze, and Paul Scott. Durham, U.K.: Durham Modern Languages Series, 2001. 39–52.

———. *Marginalité, sexualité, contrôle dans le cinéma français contemporain.* Paris: L'Harmattan, 2000a.

———. "Negotiating Conformity: Tales of Ordinary Evil." *France in Focus: Film and National Identity.* Ed. Elizabeth Ezra and Sue Harris. Oxford: Berg, 2000b. 195–205.

Beugnet, Martine, and Jane Sillars. "*Beau Travail:* Time, Space, and Myths of Identity." *Studies in French Cinema* 1.3 (2001): 166–73.

Bjornson, Richard. *The African Quest for Freedom and Identity: Cameroonian Writing and the National Experience.* Bloomington: Indiana University Press, 1991.

Bonvoisin, Samra, and Mary-Anne Brault-Wiart. *L'Aventure du premier film.* Paris: B. Barrault, 1989.

Bouquet, Stéphane. "Claire Denis, les années sauvages de Nénette et Boni." *Cahiers du Cinéma* 501 (April 1996): 55–58.

———. "U.S. Go Home (Review)." *Cahiers du Cinéma* 485 (November 1994): 28.

Bouzet, Ange-Dominique. "Le Coq, symboliquement, c'est très lié à l'homme." *Libération* [Paris], September 5, 1990: 21–22.

Breillat, Catherine, and Claire Denis. "Le Ravissement de Marie: Dialogue entre Catherine Breillat et Claire Denis." *Cahiers du Cinéma* 534 (April 1999): 42–46.

Brody, Jeb. *The Lifetime Series: Claire Denis.* March 2000. 06/04/03 <http://www.ammi.org/calendar/SeriesArchives/DenisSeries.htm>.

Callahan, Vicki. "Zones of Anxiety: Movement, Musidora, and the Crime Serials of Louis Feuillade." *Velvet Light Trap* 37 (Spring 1996): 37–50.

Cardullo, Bert. "Black and White, in Color." *Hudson Review* 42.4 (Winter 1990): 613–20.

Chutkow, David. "Angry Africa Seen in French Girl's Eyes." *San Francisco Chronicle,* April 16, 1989, Sunday Arts: 29.

Le Cinéma vers son second siècle. Métropolis. ARTE. August 20, 1995.

Colmant, Marie. "Man No Run (Review)." *Libération* [Paris], October 18, 1989: 18.

Colpin, Françoise. "Claire, une femme de son époque." *Regards* 20 (January 1997). 13/05/03 <http://www.regards.fr/archives/1997/199701/199701cit04.html>.

Cooper, Sarah. "Je Sais Bien, Mais Quand Même: Fetishism, Envy, and the Queer Pleasures of *Beau Travail.*" *Studies in French Cinema* 1.3 (2001): 174–82.

Darbois, Dominique. *Agossou, le petit africain.* Paris: F. Nathan, 1955.

———. *Hassan, l'enfant du désert.* Paris: F. Nathan, 1960.

———. *Rikka, la petite balinaise.* Paris: F. Nathan, 1957.

Darke, Chris. "Desire Is Violence." *Sight and Sound* 10.7 (July 2000): 16–18.

Day of British Cinema. 1995. 20/08/03 <http://www.loustal.nl/day of british cinema.htm>

del Rio, Elana. "Performing the Narrative of Seduction: Claire Denis' *Beau Travail.*" *Kinoeye* 3.7 (June 9, 2003). 22/09/03 <http://www.kinoeye.org/03/07/delrio07.php>.

Denis, Claire. "Contribution to the Film-Makers Panel." *Screening Europe: Image and Identity in Contemporary European Cinema.* Ed. Duncan Petrie. London: British Film Institute, 1992. 66–67.

Denis, Claire, and Jean-Pôl Fargeau. "I Can't Sleep." *Scenario* 3.2 (Summer 1997): 52–81.

Denis, Claire, and Agnès Godard, audio commentary. *Trouble Every Day.* DVD, 2001.

Denis, Claire, and Kent Jones, audio commentary. *Friday Night.* DVD. Wellspring, 2003.

Denorme, Vincent, and Emmanuel Douin. "Travelling Light (Interview with Claire Denis)." *Modam* [Paris], Autumn 2001: 20–26.

Domarchi, Jean, Jean-Luc Godard, Jacques Doniol-Valcroze, and Pierre Kast. "*Hiroshima mon amour.*" *Cahiers du Cinéma: The 1950s. Neo-Realism, Hollywood, New Wave.* Ed. Jim Hillier. Cambridge: Harvard University Press, 1959; rpt. and translation, 1985. 59–70.

Dundes, Alan. "Gallus as Phallus: A Psychoanalytic Cross-Cultural Consideration of the Cockfight as Fowl Play." *The Cockfight: A Casebook.* Ed. Alan Dundes. Madison: University of Wisconsin Press, 1994. 241–82.

Everett, Wendy. "Timetravel and European Film." *European Identity in Cinema.* Ed. Wendy Everett. Exeter, England: Intellect Books, 1996. 103–11.

Fanon, Frantz. *Black Skins, White Masks.* New York: Grove Press, 1952; English trans. 1967 by Charles Lam Markmann.

Festival du vent. Interviewer Philippe Lefait. Le Cercle. France 2, Paris. October 27, 1998. 85 minutes.

Forbes, Jill. *The Cinema in France: After the New Wave.* Bloomington: Indiana University Press, 1993.

Frodon, Jean-Michel. "Claire Denis ou l'art du partage." *Le Monde* [Paris], January 30, 1997: Culture-Cinéma: 1.

———. "Il s'agit de s'aventurer au-devant d'une forme." *Le Monde* [Paris], July 11, 2001: 3.

Frois, Emmanuelle, and Dominique Borde. "Réalisatrice d'un Film Choc, *Trouble Every Day,* avec Béatrice Dalle et Vincent Gallo." *Le Figaro* [Paris], July 11, 2001: Culture.

Fuller, Charles, Hortense Fuller, and Jean-Marie Ahanda. *A History of Bikutsi Music in Cameroon.* 1997. Africa Sounds. 15/11/03 <http://www.africasounds.com/history_of_bikutsi.htm>.

Garbarz, Franck. "*Nénette et Boni:* Mère, pourquoi nous as-tu abandonnés?" *Positif* 432 (February 1997): 38–39.

Geertz, Clifford. "Deep Play: Notes on the Balinese Cockfight." *The Cockfight: A Casebook.* Ed. Alan Dundes. Madison: University of Wisconsin Press, 1972; rpt. 1994. 94–132.

Gili, Jean A. "Entretien avec Claire Denis sur *Chocolat.*" *Positif* 328 (June 1988): 14–16.

Giuffrida, Daniela. *Jacques Rivette: La Règle du jeu.* Torino: Centre culturel français de Turin: Museo nazionale del cinema di Torino, 1991.

Godard, Jean-Luc. *Deux ou trois choses que je sais d'elle (découpage intégral).* Paris: Seuil, 1971.

Gordon, Lewis R., T. Denean Sharpley-Whiting. *Fanon: A Critical Reader.* Oxford: Blackwell Publishers, 1996.

Grant, Catherine. "Recognizing *Billy Budd* in *Beau Travail:* Epistemology and Hermeneutics of an Auteurist 'Free' Adaptation." *Screen* 43.1 (Spring 2002): 57–73.

Grugeau, Gérard. "La Vie est une pizza." *24 Images* 88–89 (Autumn 1997): 85.

Guilloux, Michel. "Claire Denis: De l'Amour est passé." *L'Humanité* [Paris], January 29, 1997: 28.

Hadas, Moses. *The Stoic Philosophy of Seneca.* Gloucester, Mass.: Peter Smith, 1965.

Hall, Stuart. "European Cinema on the Verge of a Nervous Breakdown." *Screening Europe: Image and Identity in Contemporary European Cinema.* Ed. Duncan Petrie. London: British Film Institute, 1992. 45–53.

Hart, Adam. "Interview: Claire Denis." *24 Frames Per Second* (2003). 15/11/03 <http://www.24framespersecond.com/writings/writing.php?writing=clairedenis>.

Hayward, Susan. "Claire Denis' Films and the Post-Colonial Body—with Special Reference to *Beau Travail* (1999)." *Studies in French Cinema* 1.3 (2001): 159–65.

———. "Claire Denis's 'Post-Colonial' Films and Desiring Bodies." *L'Esprit Createur* 42.3 (Fall 2002a): 39–49.

———. "Reading Masculinities in Claire Denis's *Chocolat.*" *New Cinemas: Journal of Contemporary Film* 1.2 (2002b): 120–27.

Heymann, Daniel. "*S'en Fout la mort* de Claire Denis: L'homme est un coq pour l'homme." *Le Monde* [Paris], September 6, 1990: Le monde des arts et des spectacles: 23.

Himes, Chester. *The Quality of Hurt.* Garden City, N.Y.: Doubleday, 1972.

Holden, Stephen. "Erotic Horror with Enough Gore to Distress Dracula." *New York Times,* March 1, 2002: B: 24.

Hurst, Heike. "Entretien avec Claire Denis." *Jeune Cinéma* 242 (March–April 1997): 23–27.

Interview with Claire Denis. 2. Journal du cinéma de Mercredi. Canal +. April 10, 1996.

James, Nick. "Tender Is the Tailback Night." *Sight and Sound* 13.9 (September 2003): 8–9.

Jones, Kent. "Claire Denis." *Visions Magazine* 8 (1992): 10–15.

———. "The Dance of the Unknown Soldier." *Film Comment* 36.3 (May–June 2000): 26–27.

Jorion, Paul. "Dans le Ventre de la nounou cosmique." *Libération* [Paris], June 15, 1988, Idées: 9.

Jousse, Thierry, interviewer. Part 1. *Enfance africaine: Entretien avec Claire Denis (1ère émission). A voix nue: Grands entretiens d'hier et aujourd'hui.* Radio France. France Culture, Paris. May 13, 2002. 25 minutes.

———, interviewer. Part 2. *Autour de la musique: Entretien avec Claire Denis (2me émission). A voix nue: Grands entretiens d'hier et aujourd'hui.* Radio France. France Culture, Paris. May 14, 2002. 25 minutes.

———, interviewer. Part 3. *Dans l'Oeil du cyclone: Entretien avec Claire Denis (3me émission). A voix nue: Grands entretiens d'hier et aujourd'hui.* Radio France. France Culture, Paris. May 15, 2002. 25 minutes.

———, interviewer. Part 4. *L'Intrus: Entretien avec Claire Denis (4me émission). A voix nue: Grands entretiens d'hier et aujourd'hui.* Radio France. France Culture, Paris. May 16, 2002. 25 minutes.

———, interviewer. Part 5. *Vendredi soir: Entretien avec Claire Denis (5me émission). A voix nue: Grands entretiens d'hier et aujourd'hui.* Radio France. France Culture, Paris. May 17, 2002. 25 minutes.

———. "Jeux Africains." *Cahiers du Cinéma* 407–8 (May 1988): 132–33.

Jousse, Thierry, and Frédéric Strauss. "Entretien avec Claire Denis." *Cahiers du Cinéma* 479–80 (May 1994): 24–30.

Kaplan, E. Ann. *Looking for the Other.* New York: Routledge, 1997.

Kipp, Jeremiah. "Claire Denis." *Planet,* May 2003: 38–39.

Lalanne, Jean-Marc, and Jérôme Larcher. "'Je me reconnais dans un cinéma qui fait confiance à la narration plastique': Entretien avec Claire Denis." *Cahiers du Cinéma* 545 (April 2000): 50–53.

Lefort, Gérard. "Claire Denis sous l'adolescence." *Libération* [Paris], January 29, 1997: 33.

Lifshitz, Sébastien. *Claire Denis, la vagabonde.* Fémis, 1995. 45 minutes.

Lippe, Richard. "Claire Denis and Masculinity: *Beau Travail.*" *CineAction* 51 (2000): 63–65.

Loustal, Jacques. *Duo.* Paris: L'Atelier Médicis, 1994.

Marker, Cynthia. "Sleepless in Paris: *J'ai Pas Sommeil* (Denis, 1993)." *French Cinema in the 1990s: Continuity and Difference.* Ed. Phil Powrie. Oxford: Oxford University Press, 1999. 137–47.

Maule, Rosanna. "Women's Authorial Practices in European National Cinemas." *Iris* 28 (Autumn 1999): 123–38.

Maveyraud, Cécilie. "Les Années surboum." *Télérama* 2337 (October 26, 1994): 90–91.

McGowan, Todd. "Resisting the Lure of Ultimate Enjoyment: Claire Denis' *J'ai Pas Sommeil* (1994)." *Kinoeye* 3.7 (June 9, 2003). 22/09/03 <http://www.kinoeye.org/03/07/mcgowan07.php>.

Medina, Ramon. *Interview with Claire Denis.* November 2001. 04/06/03 <http://worshipguitars.org/clairedenis/index.html>.

Met, Philipe. "Looking for Trouble: The Dialectics of Lack and Excess (Claire Denis' *Trouble Every Day* [2001])." *Kinoeye* 3.7 (June 9, 2003). 22/09/03 <http://www.kinoeye.org/03/07/met07.php>.

"Le Monstre." *Paris Match,* December 18, 1987.

Morgan, Janice. "The Spatial Politics of Racial and Cultural Identity in Claire Denis' *Chocolat.*" *Quarterly Review of Film and Video* 20.2 (April–June 2003): 145–58.

Mudede, Charles. "City of Monsters: Claire Denis Reactivates the Underworld." *The Stranger,* March 3, 2002. May 29, 2003 <http://www.thestranger.com/2002–03–21.film.html>.

Nancy, Jean-Luc. *L'Intrus.* Paris: Editions Galilée, 2000.

Neroni, Hilary. "Lost in Fields of Interracial Desire: Claire Denis's *Chocolat* (1988)." *Kinoeye* 3.7 (June 9, 2003). 22/09/03 <http://www.kinoeye.org/03/07/neroni07.php>.

Ortoli, Philippe. *Nénette et Boni.* Paris: Bibliothèque du film et de l'image (BIFI), 2002.

Oster, Corinne. "Decoding Unreadable Spaces: Claire Denis' *J'ai Pas Sommeil* (1994)." *Kinoeye* 3.7 (June 9, 2003). 22/09/03 <http://www.kinoeye.org/03/07/oster07.php>.

Padis, Marc-Olivier. "Comment faire son deuil des trente glorieuses?" *Esprit* 225 (October 1996): 31–42.

Pantel, Monique. "Line Renaud: 'Maman, seule avec le monstre.'" *France-Soir* [Paris], May 16, 1994: 3.

Perlmutter, Ruth. "Breakdown at the Borders." *Deep Focus: A Film Quarterly* 3–4 (1998): 59–62.

Péron, Didier. "Claire Denis en eaux 'trouble.'" *Libération,* March 8, 2000. 28/2/01 <http://www.liberation.fr/cinema/archives/tournages/20000308.html>.

Petrie, Duncan, ed. *Screening Europe: Image and Identity in Contemporary European Cinema.* London: British Film Institute, 1992.

Portuges, Catherine. "*Le Colonial Féminin:* Women Directors Interrogate French Cinema." *Cinema, Colonialism, Postcolonialism: Perspectives from the French and Francophone World.* Ed. Dina Sherzer. Austin: University of Texas Press, 1996. 80–102.

Powrie, Phil, ed. *French Cinema in the 1990s: Continuity and Difference.* New York: Oxford University Press, 1999.

Reid, Mark A. "Interview with Claire Denis: Colonial Observations." *Jump Cut* 40 (1996): 67–73.

Reisinger, Deborah Streifford. "French Literary and Cinematic Response to the Contemporary Fait Divers: Discursive Struggles and Resistance (Claire Denis, Bernard-Marie Koltes)." Ph.D. diss., Dept. of Romance Languages, University of North Carolina–Chapel Hill, 2000. *AAT 3007873* (2001): 309.

Renouard, Jean-Philippe, and Lise Wajeman. "Ce poids d'ici-bas: Entretien avec Claire Denis." *Vacarme* 14 (January 2001). Interview. 03/04/02 <http://www.vacarme.eu.org/article84.html>.

"Report on *Trouble Every Day.*" *Nulle part ailleurs cinéma.* Canal +. May 13, 2001.

Rivette, Jacques. "De l'Abjection." *Cahiers du Cinéma* 126 (December 1961): 54–55.

———. *Trois films fantômes de Jacques Rivette.* Paris: Cahiers du Cinéma, 2002.

Romney, Jonathan. "Claire Denis Interviewed by Jonathan Romney." *Guardian,* June 28, 2000. 04/06/03 <http://film.guardian.co.uk/interview/interview-pages/0,6737,338784,00.html>.

Rosenbaum, Jonathan. "Unsatisfied Men." *Chicago Reader,* May 26, 2000. 23/11/01 <http://www.chireader.com/movies/archives/2000/0500/000526_2.html>.

Roth, Michael S. "Africa." *American Historical Review* 95.4 (October 1990): 1118–19.

Sandars, Diana. "Chocolat." *Senses of Cinema* 17 (November–December 2001). 04/01/02 <http://www.sensesofcinema.com/contents/01/17/cteq/chocolat.html>.

Sherzer, Dina. "Race Matters and Matters of Race: Interracial Relationships in Colonial and Postcolonial Films." *Cinema, Colonialism, Postcolonialism: Perspectives from the French and Francophone World.* Ed. Dina Sherzer. Austin: University of Texas Press, 1996. 229–48.

Sotinel, Thomas. "La Cérémonie de l'effroi." *Le Monde* [Paris], July 11, 2001.

Strand, Dana. "'Dark Continents' Collide." *French Cultural Studies: Criticism at the Crossroads.* Ed. Marie-Pierre Le Hir and Dana Strand. Albany: State University of New York Press, 2000. 221–32.

———. "Film, Food and 'La Francité': From *Le Pain Quotidien* to McDo." *French Food: On the Table, on the Page, and in French Culture.* Ed. Lawrence Schehr and Allen S. Weiss. New York: Routledge, 2001. 203–20.

Strand Releasing, distributor. Press kit for *Nénette and Boni.* Interview with Claire Denis (no author). Santa Monica, California, 1997.

Strauss, Frédéric. "Féminin Colonial." *Cahiers du Cinéma* 434 (July–August 1990): 28–33.

———. "Miam-Miam." *Cahiers du Cinéma* 510 (February 1997): 64–65.

Tarr, Carrie, with Brigitte Rollet. *Cinema and the Second Sex: Women's Filmmaking in France in the 1980s and 1990s.* New York: Continuum, 2001.

Truong, Nicolas. "Claire Denis: 'Je suis un être séparé.'" *Le Monde de l'Éducation* 316 (July–August 2003): 72–77.

Turim, Maureen. *The Films of Oshima Nagisa.* Berkeley: University of California Press, 1998.

Vallaeys, Beatrice. "Faut-il faire une scène aux acteurs amateurs?" *Libération* [Paris], June 3, 1999: 16.

Villella, Fiona. "Postcolonial Cinema: *Chocolat.*" *Senses of Cinema* 1 (December 1999): French Cinema. 15/04/02 <http://www.sensesofcinema.com/contents/00/1/chocolat.html>.

Voyeux, Martine. *Ecrire contre l'oubli.* Paris: Balland, 1991.

Wellspring, distributor. Press kit for *Friday Night.* New York, 2003.

Wilson, Emma. *French Cinema since 1950: Personal Histories.* Lanham, Md.: Rowman and Littlefield, 1999.

43; and racialized point-of-view, 36–38, 43; and the tracking shot, 101–2
Cinema and the Second Sex, 27
Cocteau, Jean, 73, 117
Colin, Grégoire, xiii, 24; and *Friday Night,* 24, 124; and *Nénette and Boni,* 24, 29, 69–70, 77; and *Nice, Very Nice,* 19, 24, 136; and *U.S. Go Home,* 24, 60
Cooper, Gary, 94
Cooper, Sarah, 130n7
Corneille, Pierre, 5, 6
Costa-Gavras, Constantin, 14
Cotton Comes to Harlem (1970), 56
Courcet, Richard, 24, 143

Dacia, 69
Dalle, Béatrice, xiii, 134, 144; and *I Can't Sleep,* 24, 29, 87; and *Trouble Every Day* ix, xi, 24, 29, 105
Daney, Serge, 5–7, 143
Dani, 17
Daquin, Louis, 13
Darbois, Dominique, 11
Del Rio, Elana, 1
Demme, Jonathan, 82
Demy, Jacques, 73
Denis, Claire: appearances in films by other directors, 4–6, 31–32, 132; and collaboration with actors, 24–25, 104, 132; and collaboration with writers, editors, and cinematographers, xi, 23–25, 82, 85, 132, 144; and colonialism xi, 7, 10–12, 80–81; and contemporary French filmmakers, 9, 21–23, 31–32; and decolonization, xi, 12; and female authorship, xi, 9, 25–27, 144–45; and Paris, 12, 20; and "political correctness," 28, 82; and race, 25, 28–29; training and early career, 13–14, 15. *See also* individual films
De Palma, Brian, 109
Depardon, Raymond, 136
Derrière, Le, 122
Descas, Alex, 21, 28; and *A propos d'une déclaration,* 24; and *Duo,* 18, 24; and *I Can't Sleep,* 29, 87; and *Nénette and Boni,* 24, 28; and *No Fear, No Die,* 24,

48, 58; and *Trouble Every Day* ix, 29, 105
Devil, Probably, The (1977), 140
Dommartin, Solveig, 24, 27, 53
Doniol-Valcroze, Jacques, 103
Down By Law (1986), 33
Driver, Sara, 16, 133
Duo (1995), 18, 24
Duras, Marguerite, 103
Duvivier, Julien, 94

Ecrire contre l'oubli, 16, 37
Egoyan, Atom, 109
En avoir (ou pas), 31–32

Fanon, Frantz, 51–53, 56
Fantômas, 117
Fargeau, Jean-Pôl, 15, 23, 26; and *Beau Travail,* 92; and *Chocolat,* 36; and *I Can't Sleep,* 82, 142; and *L'Intrus,* 131; *Nénette and Boni,* 69; and *Trouble Every Day,* 108
FEMIS (Fondation Européenne des Métiers de L'Image et du Son), 13
Femme du boulanger, La, 73
Ferrara, Abel, 109
Feuillade, Louis, 117
Fillières, Hélène, 124
France-Soir, 82
Friday Night (Vendredi Soir), xii, xiii, 19, 23, 117–29; and casting, 8; and Emmanuèle Bernheim's novel, 118–22, 123; and free indirect style, 121; and Paris, 20, 32, 117, 123, 127
Frodon, Jean-Michel, 31

Gabin, Jean, 93–94, 122
Gallo, Vincent: and *Keep It For Yourself,* 24, 108, 133; and *Nénette and Boni,* 24, 76; and *Trouble Every Day,* ix, 24, 105; and *U.S. Go Home,* 66–67, 108
Gentle Creature, A (1969), 116
Godard, Agnès, 15, 16, 17, 23, 26; and *Beau Travail,* 92–93, 101; and *Nénette and Boni,* 69
Godard, Jean-Luc, 16, 60, 96; *La Chinoise,* 20–21; *Le Petit Soldat,* 93–95; on

the tracking shot, 103–4; *Two or Three Things I Know About Her* (1967), 139; *Vivre sa vie*, 21, 99

Golubeva, Katerina, 82

Good Machine, 16, 108

Grandperret, Patrick, 92

Greenaway, Peter, 133

Hanks, Tom, 82

Hartley, Hal, 136

Hayashi, Kaizo, 133

Himes, Chester, *The Quality of Hurt*, 56–57

Hinchcliffe, Dickon, 23

Hiroshima mon amour (1959), 103

Holden, Stephen, 107

Hoop Skirt, The (La Robe à cerceau) [1991], 17–18, 20

Houri, Alice, 24, 133–34; and *Nénette and Boni*, 24, 29, 69; and *U.S. Go Home*, 24, 60

Hugo, Victor, 114

Ibrahim, Abdullah, 23, 45, 85

I Can't Sleep (J'ai pas sommeil), 26, 29, 59, 80–92, 93; and gay sexuality, xiii, 81; and Martinique, 84, 87, 89, 93; and Murat, Jean-Marie, 82–83; and music, 82–86, 89, 93; and post-colonialism, 8, 19–20; and the Thierry Paulin case, 81–82, 87, 141–43; and the tracking shot, 88–92, 104; and touch, xi, 129

IDHEC (Institut des Hautes Etudes Cinematographiques), 13–14

Imamura, Shohei, 143–44

In My Room, 12

Intentions of Murder, 143–44

In the Realm of Passion, 19, 136–37

Irma Vep (1996), 109

Jacques Rivette, le veilleur (1990), 5–7, 15

Jarmusch, Jim, 14, 33

Jazz Passenger, 133

Jeanson, Francis, 20

Jones, Kent, 95

Jorion, Paul, 41, 101

Kahn, Cédric, 129

Kali, 85, 89, 93

Kapo, 104

Karina, Anna, 95, 99

Kasander, Kees, 133

Keep It For Yourself (1990), 7, 15–16

Khemir, Nacer, 136

Kiberlain, Sandrine, 31

Killing of a Chinese Bookie (1976), 57–58

Laburthe-Tolra, Philippe, 3–5

La Fontaine, Jean de, 60

Lavant, Denis, 94

L'eau froide, 129n3

Leclerc, Ginette, 73

Leconte, Patrice, 16

Le Fanu, Sheridan, 109

Lemercier, Valerie, xi, 8, 122

Les Parents Terribles, 73

Libération, 40

Library Love, 133

Lifshitz, Sébastien, 10

Lindon, Vincent, 8, 121–22

L'Intrus (book), xiii, 20, 30, 131

L'Intrus (film), xiii, 131

Loiret-Caille, Florence, 124

Lola (1961), 73

Lounge Lizards, 133

Loustal, Jacques, 18

Lumière Brothers, 33

Lurie, John, 16, 133

Lvovsky, Noémie, 32

Makavejev, Dusan, 14

Man From the Moon, 133

Man No Run (1989), 2–5, 7, 9, 15, 48. See *also* Têtes Brûlées, Les

Marley, Bob, *Buffalo Soldier*, 12, 49

Marshall, Tonie, 32, 77

Martin, Dean, 84

Masson, Laetitia, 31

May '68, 12, 14

Medina, El (2000), 31, 132

Melville, Herman, 92, 93

Monde, Le, 107

Montet, Bernardo, 93

Mouchette (1964), 140

Tarkan, 97–98

Tarr, Carrie, 27

Tavernier, Bertrand, 16

Téchiné, André, 60, 129n3, 135–36

Télé Niger, 13

Ten Minutes Older, 20

Têtes Brûlées, Les, 2–3, 32, 48. *See also Man No Run*

Tindersticks, 23–24, 111; and *Nénette and Boni,* 72, 78, 85

Tourneur, Jacques, 109

Tous les garçons et les filles de leur âge (1990), 18, 60, 129n4, 135

Trintignant, Nadine, 16

Trop de bonheur, 129

Trouble Every Day (2001), ix-x, xii, xiii, 19, 105–17; and controversy, 8, 107–8; and liminality, 110–11, 113, 117; and Paris, 105, 111, 113–17, 123, 127

Turim, Maureen, 19

Two or Three Things I Know about Her (1967), 139

Under the Sand (2000), 118

Une vie de boy, 35–36, 127

U.S. Go Home (1994), xii, 18–19, 20, 59–69; brother/sister relations in, 60, 96, 130n4; and dance, 60, 62–64, 67; and music, 60, 64–68, 85, 128; relationship with *Nénette and Boni,* 69, 72, 73, 77, 80

Vampires, Les, 117

Vénus beauté (institut), 32

Vers Nancy (2002), 20–21, 30

Vessey, Tricia, ix, xi, 105

Vigo, Jean, 19, 23, 136

Visitors, The (1993), 122

Vivre sa vie (My Life to Live), 21, 99

Wall, Jeff, 109

Washington, Denzel, 82

Wellman, William, 94

Wenders, Wim, 14–15, 31, 53

Whiter Shade of Pale, 85

Wiazemsky, Anne, 20–21; and *U.S. Go Home,* 23, 60

Wilson, Brian, 12

Wilson, Emma, 22

Wings of Desire, 23, 53

Workers Leaving the Factory (1895), 33

Yardbirds, The, 12, 60, 65

Young, Neil, *Safeway Cart,* 12

Judith Mayne is Distinguished Humanities Professor and
Professor of French and Women's Studies at the Ohio State
University.